'A swashbuckling collection of stories based on McLennan's extraordinarily itinerant life . . . great yarns, great fun' *Times*

'These tales are as much about a way of life as they are chronicles of one man's travels. McLennan has a goldmine of experiences to draw on, and his life is enviable in many ways. It's certainly macho; but in the celebration of this lifestyle, in beautiful prose often reminiscent of Hemingway, the book comes alive' *Time Out*

'Not only has he managed to recall vividly a series of rough-and-ready tales . . . he has done so, entertainingly, with a minimum of soul-searching and a maximum of no-nonsense storytelling' *Times Literary Supplement*

'These "true stories" combine a visceral, casual lyricism with an easy, honest, punch-your-weight directness' *Scotsman*

'McLennan's affection for those he meets allows us glimpses of kindness and honesty that might be overlooked by more fastidious writers. The juxtaposition of the coarse, uncompromising lives he encounters and the arrestingly beautiful landscapes they are lived in makes for interesting reading.' *Financial Times*

Wayne McLennan was born in New South Wales, Australia in 1954. He now lives with his wife in Amsterdam and runs a business in Estonia. *Rowing to Alaska* is his first book.

ROWING TO ALASKA

and other true stories

WAYNE McLENNAN

Granta Books

London

Granta Publications, 2/3 Hanover Yard, Noel Road, London N1 8BE

First published in Great Britain by Granta Books 2004
This edition published by Granta Books 2005

A CIP catalogue record for this book is available
from the British Library.

1 3 5 7 9 10 8 6 4 2

Typeset by M Rules
Printed and bound in Great Britain by
Mackays of Chatham plc

For my father, Les Geale: thanks mate.

Many thanks to Maarten Carbo and Carolina van Tuyll van Serooskerken who were the first to see something worthwhile in my writing.

Our nature lies in movement, complete calm is death.

PASCAL

CONTENTS

INTRODUCTION

It was a hard winter in Estonia in 1998. Snow lay feet thick on the ground for months, trees bent double with its weight. When they cleared the roads only ice tracks were left.

I moved to Estonia with my Dutch wife so that she could write a book. We bought a large wooden house that stood in a bare field and was surrounded by grey, naked pine trees. The house, which had previously been the village school, was badly insulated, letting the icy north winds weave through its cracks as easily as water saturates paper. We drank abundant amounts of Moldavian brandy and Estonian Vodka, lived on fatty sausage, pork, potatoes and cabbage, and I ate blocks and blocks of chocolate, which I have since read is craved by depressed people.

Each morning, I crawled from under a great mound of coverings, threw on a heavy full-length coat over my long underwear, pulled on knee-length leather boots, and settled a Russian military fur cap over my head, pulling the flaps down tightly over my ears, and – complaining – ploughed through the snow to the barn at the back of the house to collect firewood for our two massive brick-lined, cast-iron stoves.

I then spent the next three hours lighting, banking and

nurturing the fires, until the flames had turned to bright glowing embers. Only then could I close off the air vents, confident it would not smoke, and there was enough heat to keep the stove-bricks furnace-hot, and so the house warm. In the afternoons, I would split firewood, and then there was always the drinking.

When I complained about boredom, my wife told me to write something. 'You're always telling stories, write them down,' she said.

'But I can't spell,' I told her, 'and besides, I've never written anything before.'

'Try,' she said.

And then she reminded me that I had written her six letters, and then I remembered the four I had written my mother. And so I wrote my first story and re-wrote it and then re-wrote it again, and continued.

Estonia was the last stop in many years of moving about. I left my homeland Australia for London with a mate when I was twenty-three years old. In Australia, I had worked for three and a half tedious years as a bank teller, I had been a bread carter, a barman, store man, vineyard labourer, and a pro boxer, but not a good one. I hoped the trip would lead to something, although my notion of what that might be was vague. I knew the alternative would be to settle down, but with less than impressive school results, to what? My family had all been coal miners, but the mines were closing down, and mining had never been in my plans.

In London, we bought a van and toured Europe, following in the tyre tracks of countless other colonials on their indeterminate romp through the Old World. Our idea had been to return home after six months, but I couldn't go. I lingered after my mate left, giving myself up to any impulse that would delay my return to Australia.

After two and a half years of working on the building sites and in the pubs of London, I moved to Seattle in the States, worked as a tree planter and dishwasher. I cleaned office buildings. I had a boat built, and along with a friend, I rowed it to Alaska.

In Alaska I found work on a salmon fishing boat, returned to Australia at the end of the season, but never meant to stay. I was still searching, and besides, something had happened to me, and I could no longer stay happily in one place for any length of time.

When I returned to Alaska, I was offered work on a boat fishing king crab in the Aleutians. Rough-weather work, cold and icy, but you could earn thirty-five thousand dollars in a season as a deckhand. Exactly what I needed. My boat ran aground on the way to its northern port of Dutch Harbour, where I was to meet it, and missed the season. I found work in the building trade until the snows and cold closed us down in January, and I headed to Costa Rica.

It had been a *National Geographic* magazine article that had tempted me south.

I read that it was a democracy, that it had no army, that the girls were beautiful. There were pictures. Nicaragua and El Salvador were at war at the time, Honduras was a military dictatorship. Costa Rica was paradise.

There was a gold rush going on, and like a lot of other people, I got caught up in it. I worked in the rivers for more than two years. At times I bought and sold gold, keeping my head at all times, just above water. It was in Costa Rica that I met my Dutch wife, and it was because of her that I moved to Holland with my last $800. But labouring work was plentiful in Amsterdam in those days.

We made a trip to Australia later that same year and worked our way slowly around that continent. While my wife wrote, I found good employment in the meat works in Broome in Western Australia's far north, and was tempted to stay, but it was only the temptation that comes from familiarity, and that wasn't strong enough to keep me.

On our return trip to Amsterdam, I bought samples of silk in China, and found that I had stumbled upon an opportunity. I opened a successful shop, McLennan's Pure Silk, travelling twice a year to China and Thailand to buy new stock. But then I sold the business because of a panic that comes to most men at a certain time in life, and set off again.

I headed back to Costa Rica, but it had changed too much as things always do when looked at through older eyes, and I ended up in Nicaragua. The war had finished, it was a democracy of sorts, I had a boat built, went fishing for a couple of years, got involved with the local boxing, and then it was time for Estonia.

My stories are true. Most of the people mentioned are still mates, and I still see them on a regular basis.

ROWING TO ALASKA

THE TENT

Our summers always burned hot like a blacksmith's fire, baking your mouth as you breathed deeply, leaving you hunting for oxygen in the dry brittle air. The light was so hard that you were forced to narrow your eyes and squint in order to stop blinking against the glare. You were supposed to move more slowly in our summers, rest often, cherish the shade. But we never did, we were young.

When March arrived, the first month of autumn in the Southern Hemisphere, the days had already cooled and became only warm and pleasant. In the night you could sleep easily, unbothered. The colours of living things were still faded and lifeless but a little rain and a weakened sun would quickly change that. March was also a time of anticipation, of excitement. It was the month that brought us three days of worldly sensations. It was in March that the country show came to town.

The show would bring our men away from the land to exhibit their cattle. The crowds could admire powerful-chested bulls with wide sloping foreheads, or cows with large milk-swollen udders being led around the show ring by proud, slightly embarrassed farmers. Merino sheep were shown at their best: fat, woolly, white.

The town women would make their most delicious jams and let them be judged on their colour, texture and taste. Pies and cakes were baked to see whose was the tastiest. The biggest and best vegetables that the region produced were displayed for all to see: squash so large and misshapen that you wondered how they could be so admired, pumpkins too big to lift, watermelons with perfect spherical shapes that had been nicked through the skin to show a red ripeness that promised sweetness and more sweetness.

We had wood chopping contests where men with strong shoulders wearing long white pants and tight white singlets hacked away at blocks of wood with axes so sharp they could scrape the hairs off their arm with only a little spit for lubrication. Chips flew from their blades so thickly and with such force that it was dangerous to stand too near.

There were trotting events: tightly muscled horses pulling small buggies that were no more than seats mounted on springs attached to wheels, carrying drivers who would race around a circular track anticlockwise, churning the dust left over from our summer into a heavy swirling brown cloak which camouflaged the horses until it became a guess as to who was leading.

We had equestrian competitions where men and women in red coats and peaked hard caps sat stiffly on groomed and pampered horses that danced with unnatural gaits. Jumping events where rider and horse flew together higher and higher, and we had our cowboys and cowgirls.

I was not a cowboy, sons of coal miners generally were not, but there were exceptions and my cousin Billy was one. Billy's father was a cowboy, a coal-mining cowboy. A man who knew horses as well as he understood the work he had to do a half a mile below the ground.

My cousin had entered most events. His horse, a man-sized bay mare called Lady, was fast and tough. I knew through experience that she had a playful streak with anyone not born to the saddle. Billy was a fearless rider and together they made a hard team to beat. I sat watching from the top rail of the wooden fence that ran the circumference of our show grounds as Billy caressed Lady's neck, whispered in her ear, and then slowly, very slowly, saddled and cinched her. Behind me, on the far side of the wooden grandstand that was built to overlook the showground, came the sounds and smells of the travelling carnival, the other part of our show, the frivolous part. But first the cowboys had to ride.

The first event was the barrel race. As soon as the signal was given to go, Lady flew forward, turning tightly in and out of the barrels that had been placed three metres apart. Billy leaning slightly in the direction that he wanted Lady to turn, laying his reins in the same direction American-style. There were ten other riders in the race, all racing parallel, all lying across the necks of their mounts, turning them in, turning them out, their hats flying from their heads, waltzing with the breeze, pirouetting, bowing, and floating to ground before the horses had reached the first barrel. Billy pulled hard at the end and the last short gallop made him and Lady the winner.

He dismounted, smiling and hooting, excited from the ride and win, his checked shirt stained brown from sweat and dust. But it wasn't long before he was mounted, waiting, ready to ride again.

In the flag race you were meant to ride hard to the end of a line of thin poles that had been hammered into the rough dry ground, swing your horse around the last one, while at the same time plucking a flag from the top of the pole, gallop back to the start, and drop the flag into a hessian bag. Then back again to the next last pole, and so on, until all the flags were in the bag. Billy was good, Lady fast. Two events and two wins: it was Billy's year. We were both fifteen.

The next race Billy had entered was the rescue race, but before the event started he ambled slowly over to me cowboy-style, a serious look on his face. 'I need you to jump for me in the next race.'

'What happened to your mate Johnny, he's your jumper?' I replied slowly, suspiciously.

'Johnny's gone and broke his arm.'

'Practising for the rescue race?' I asked, bringing a smirk to Billy's face.

'No mate, it happened at ballet practice. You're going to have to jump.'

Billy was a cowboy and I was not part of his world of horses. I had no idea what a jumper in a rescue race was supposed to do, but that didn't seem to worry Billy.

'You'll be right, mate,' was all he would say to my enquiries, 'you'll be right.'

'Yeah,' I answered, 'like Johnny.'

As I stood watching Billy charge down on me at full gallop, lying so far over Lady's head he looked like he was belly down on the horse's back, my courage faltered. I moved a step to my right, one to the left, and then contemplated a full flight in the direction of the grandstand, but in the end, decided on holding my ground, hoping Billy could steer the horse around me and not through me.

This was the rescue race as it had been loosely explained to me only minutes before. 'Stand your ground,' Billy had said, 'I'll canter up to you.' Canter, no mention of full-blooded gallop. 'When I swing Lady around you, grab the pommel of the saddle and swing up onto her back behind me. I'll help pull you up and off we canter to the finish.' Canter again. Billy had made it sound so easy.

It was too late before I realized that Billy was not the faultless rider I had always thought him. Lady's head slammed into my left shoulder spinning me. Billy reefed on the reins, twisting Lady around me, through me.

'Grab the saddle,' he screamed through my pain, 'grab the saddle, mate.'

As I slid my hand between Lady's sweating back and the front of the saddle, missing the pommel completely, Billy dug his heels into Lady's side and her front feet lifted just a little from the ground as she leaped forward. I was forced to run beside her like a circus trick rider before I balanced enough to swing onto her back behind Billy. Another few paces and we were in full gallop, Billy again riding horizontally with me hanging on and hanging on, heading towards the line a quarter of a mile away. As we crossed Lady slowed a little, I eased my unbreakable grip on Billy's shoulders, and glanced to either side. We had won – yards separated us from the sweat-lathered horse that had come in second. We had beaten twelve other riders. Billy turned to me solemnly and said, 'Good win, just one more race and we've got it.' He had failed to mention that this was just a heat and we would need to race again against the winners of the next heat. My excitement died.

The next time Lady came hurtling down on me I was ready, experienced. As Billy turned Lady around me I turned with them, locked my left hand around the pommel and swung onto her sweating slippery back. Even before Lady came to a full gallop I was squealing with delight, looking around at the other riders lying over the necks of their horses, at their jumpers clinging, encouraging. As we raced ahead, I bought my newly borrowed cowboy hat from my head and started swinging it wildly; a cowboy for a moment.

Billy couldn't stop talking as he unsaddled Lady. 'We were flying,' he shouted, 'flying.' And I knew we were flying. As I thought about it, I realized how smooth Lady had been, as if she

7

too were riding and not being ridden. I didn't remember feeling her hooves pounding on the hard ground or any exertion in her breathing, just a speed that was natural and came effortlessly.

The events had finished for the night, it was time to get Lady home, brushed down, fed and watered. I watched Billy leave, he had thrown a blanket over Lady's back and he carried the saddle on his own, he had set his hat high on his forehead, his legs bowed a little, people made way for them.

I left the show ring soon after Billy and headed for the back of the grandstand. The smell of horse manure and sweat-hot animal clung to my clothes leaving me feeling strangely secure, confident, as if they had always been part of my life.

When I reached side-show alley the aroma of fairy floss and freshly made toffee apples filled my nostrils and made my mouth moist, wet at the corners. Lights flashed and punched at the darkness, bells rang, drums beat. My nerves tingled with pleasure. The coloured lights from the giant Ferris wheel which towered above the world were sparkling like precious gems, radiant against the black night sky. I walked easily, astonished at the richness about me.

The alley was formed by two rows of attractions, creating a dusty winding road where people strolled, turning this way and that, caught up in the spell of the bright colours, noise and promise.

On one side of the alley was a row of grotesque-looking porcelain clown heads with large gaping red mouths. The heads turned slowly from left to right, inviting you to drop delicate white balls into their mouths. The balls would then drop down through the throat, finally spitting out into a numbered lane where you could win a prize, or not.

Next came a merry-go-round with horses carved from wood, painted, gilded and impaled with golden poles that ran from roof to floor, and let them dance up and down in time with the music while slowly travelling around and around.

We had rides where people sat on metal horses that were attached by cables to a revolving circular roof, turning faster and faster until you flew horizontally above the heads of the gaping audience. Bumper cars, a ride called the octopus that turned your stomach and pumped your heart, the ghost train, that never scared anybody over five years old, and we had my favourite: Jimmy Sharman's boxing tent.

I could hear the spruiker – the caller – throwing out challenges to 'any mug brave enough to step into the ring with my fighters' and promising ten dollars if he could last three rounds. I could feel the drum that they pounded to get your attention – 'Boom, boom, boom' – long before I reached the tent, long before I saw the fighters standing on a raised platform stripped to the waist, arms folded, glaring down at the audience.

Behind the boxers, stretching the length of the tent, hung a two-metre-high canvas mural painted with hard strong colours. Dave Sands, Les Darcy, Ron Richards, George Barnes, Vic Patrick, Jimmy Carruthers, all the greats of Australian boxing stared down at you smiling, arms raised in victory, or with gloved hands shaped up, ready to fight.

As I reached the tent I came against a thick crowd of men milling, listening, building up courage. The spruiker was working hard, introducing his boxers one by one. The heavier men were mostly old fighters: white men with thick middles and faces that had worked often. Past their best but still good enough to take on local boys, the yokels from the bush. Heavier men always last longer in the boxing game, the strength that comes with their heavy bodies gives them longevity even after their other skills have diminished; speed and technique are less important to a big man, but he still has to be hard, he still has to want to fight.

The lighter fighters were younger and, except for one round-shouldered boy with a long appendix scar running across his belly, Aboriginal. Coal-black, coffee and bush-honey coloured men with strong thin legs, and noses so broad they spread to the cheekbones.

Cessnock was a coal-mining town, one of the earliest European settlements in Australia. Aboriginals had long been hunted out of our area, pushed further into the bush, closer towards oblivion. Our people came out of the deep tunnels of north England and Wales, or the poverty and wretchedness of occupied Ireland. We didn't travel much, most coal miners work hard and stay with their own. We didn't see a lot of Aboriginals and we didn't understand them. Few people tried to in those days. These dark men standing on the raised platform, more sinew than muscle and with smiles so large you could easily forget their profession were stranger to us in our ignorance than any immigrant who had just arrived in our country from a faraway land across the sea.

I moved deeper into the crowd, men and boys stood staring up at the fighters, feet spread, wondering was it all worth it. Three rounds to fight against one of these tent fighters to earn ten dollars. But it wasn't about the money.

I stood next to a soldier who seemed like he wanted to fight. He was tall and tapered, a middle or light heavy I thought. His thick dark hair was worn long enough to cover the top half of his ears and was slicked down on the top and made to shine with a greasy cream. He wore long straight sideburns and if you looked at him from the side he had bumps along the bridge of his nose, from the front it was wide and bent. His eyes were smiling and he was very relaxed as he answered the spruiker, 'I'll have a go, mate. I'll take your bloody money.' The crowd roared their approval, 'Good on ya, mate, you'll do all right.' Cessnock men and boys loved Jimmy Sharman's boxing troupe.

As the caller continued his work, haranguing the locals,

matching more men, I took the time to look the soldier up and down again. He looked the part, that was for sure, and then by glancing at his feet I knew he must be able to fight, there was no doubt: he was already wearing boxing boots. Our soldier was a ring in, one of the show fighters playing the part of the local.

He was going to fight a stew: a fake fight where both fighters pull their punches, or aim the harder ones at their opponents' arms, shoulders or gloves. Often blood was drawn but without malice, just by accident, like an actor forgetting his lines. It took a lot of skill to box a stew, you had to have two good fighters in the ring. I should have realized sooner, the long hair and the sideburns were give-aways, the Aussie army wouldn't allow that.

I had heard stories about this kind of fight from my family, my coal-mining, boxing family. It happened a lot in the carnival world when good opponents couldn't be found. My uncle, who was the best of all of us, told me once, 'You had to know the fight game pretty well to tell it was not a serious fight and most country boys didn't, a little blood and a lot of swinging were enough for them. People were entertained, money was made, and nobody was hurt. It was all right.' This soldier who was not a soldier would be fighting against another member of the troupe and we would cheer for him. The drum kept beating until three more willing locals raised their hands and yelled, 'I'll have a go.'

Inside the large canvas tent a makeshift ring had been set up: ropes fashioned around a dirt floor covered with sawdust, and again by canvas. Small wooden stools had been placed in the corners to rest on between rounds, tin buckets filled with water and a large sponge stood beside the stools outside the ropes. Old white towels hung over the ropes. The tent filled with men, so many that they seemed to steal the air. The caller appeared. 'Let's have the soldier,' rose a chorus of shouts from the public who were

11

pushed together like cattle on a road train. 'Patience, in good time,' cried the caller to the gathering, most of whom were a little drunk and had no time for patience. The first fight was introduced.

In the left corner, bare footed, and wearing only a pair of jeans and a loose, soiled blue singlet that tightened as it rode over his beer gut looking for his pants, was a man called Bonk. I'd known him most of my life; a drunk, still young but nevertheless a drunk. I'd never seen him fight but I knew he was a local rough-nut, a pub brawler, and here he stood before us, ready to have a go.

His opponent was one of the old pugs, a big sandy-haired man with thick scarred eyebrows and on each biceps rough jailhouse tattoos which were so faded that they resembled smudges left when a badly coloured shirt becomes wet and leaves a dye imprint on bare skin. According to the manager, he had been a top light heavy in Queensland, one of the best produced in the bush, but you never knew.

When he came out to meet Bonk in the middle of the ring he moved a little heavily, slower than he must once have been, but his hands were shaped up and his chin was tucked neatly into his chest for protection. You could see he had done a lot of fighting.

Bonk was drunk, not falling-down drunk, just, I'm-brave-now drunk. He had a lot of mates in the audience shouting and cheering for him, willing him to fight, and this seemed to give him courage because he came out swinging. His swings unfortunately were all loose, round-armed, and were easily blocked by the tent fighter who held his gloves high, leaned away from the punches, and at the same time brought up his shoulder to deflect anything the gloves missed.

Bonk's mates in the crowd were going wild, screaming as one, 'Bonk, Bonk, Bonk.' All they understood was the attack, as far as they were concerned Bonk was murdering the tent man.

Without effort and almost unnoticed the big Queenslander bent at the knees, went under a Bonk right-hand roundhouse and came back with a short left hook that laid the Cessnock boy on his back. It had been thrown sweetly, timed perfectly, it caught Bonk moving forward, and it happened so quickly that Bonk's mates were still cheering for him as he lay still, not moving on the dirt ring floor. When they realized it was the end, just one punch needed, they started howling like dingoes in the night, mocking Bonk, laughing at Bonk. He sat up slowly, leaned to one side and vomited. His cheek had been sliced open, blood was flowing across his white face and dripping into the sick. He was lifted to his feet by the spruiker who was also the referee and walked to the fresh air at the back of the tent, given some water, his blood swabbed away. Some of the tent fighters stayed with him until he recovered. Bonk's mates were watching the next stoush.

The second fight was introduced and began quickly. It was between a local boy who was pro boxing himself but was not considered much good, and an Aboriginal boy who was lighter and much shorter. For three rounds the Cessnock fighter stayed well out of range, throwing straight lefts and rights from his greater height. They were not difficult punches to move around but the tent fighter was content to block and land the occasional counter. In the great heat of the tent, the Aboriginal boy didn't break a sweat and never stopped smiling. The management was happy that a local would earn some money: it was good for business. 'Let's hear it for the boy from Cessnock,' yelled the spruiker in his voice of gravel and honey as he paid out the money.

As our soldier climbed through the ropes, the men around me grew agitated, excited. 'He'll do all right,' I heard the man next to me whisper to his mate, 'look at the bloody muscles on him, must be all that soldier training.' They expected something from this stranger, who had been taken as one of ours, although no one could have known him.

The gloves that were used were old and worn, the type that would cut you easily. They were dark brown and when laced on our soldier's hands looked like the knobbly head of a club used for bashing in the brains of animals on ancient hunts. They stood in opposite corners of the ring, our man with his back to the tent fighter, waiting to be called to fight by the clang of the bell.

Without warning, his opponent rushed from his own corner and threw a chopping right hand that caught the soldier on the right ear dropping him to the ground like a coin falling through a hole in a worn pants pocket. The crowd roared with honest workingman's indignation and contempt at the unfairness. They yelled abuse at the tent fighter who stood towering over our man, challenging him to 'get up and fight, ya mongrel.'

The tent fighter was one of the older pros who had gone a little flabby around the middle, but only a little. It was the type of flab that comes from training between drinking, a controlled belly. His shoulders and chest were huge and knotted, uncorrupted by tattoos. His head was small, but only in comparison to his shoulders, and cropped with thinning hair bleached white from the sun. The eyebrows, which had also bleached, were almost invisible. Teeth were missing.

The crowd pushed towards the ropes, intent on helping our man, but before all control was lost the soldier stood, steady as an old strong tree, shaped his hands up, and started throwing punches hard, fast and often. The soldier was smaller but in better shape, his breathing strong, unhindered by fat. A tattoo of a woman with long dark hair that partially hid her beckoning naked body danced on his left breast with each breath that he took, and contorted violently with every left-hand punch he threw. To the delight of everybody the tent fighter went down. It was a left rip hook combination thrown fast and with purpose, but not a killing purpose if you looked carefully. Up got the tent fighter, in he came, wild-eyed, mad, down went our man, landing on his back in one motion as if hit full-on by a charging bull. Up he got, furious.

The Cessnock crowd loved it. They were breathing as heavily as the fighters, throwing as many punches, knocking down their own phantom opponents. This action went on for the entire fight. Down, up and down again, neither man getting the better of the other. By the rules of the contest the soldier had won, he had lasted the three rounds. The tent fighter was cut on the bridge of the nose but this had come from being brushed by the laces of an old glove. Both of these men were too good to hurt each other.

'Piss off, ya black Abo bastard.' Everybody in the tent heard it. Pat had screamed it in defence of his mate, who was taking a bad beating by one of the Aboriginal boys in the last fight of the night. Pat knew when he said it that it was a mistake, he knew that now he would have to fight and not in the ring with a referee.

It wasn't the fighter who had been insulted who called him outside – he was too busy finishing off Pat's mate in the ring under the roof of the hot hot tent, it was one of the other Aboriginals. That was the way these tent men were, they stood up for each other, you had to when you drifted through redneck towns with a travelling carnival. Towns where local boys were tribal. And you had to certainly if you were Aboriginal, we all understood that.

Pat belonged to Bonk's group. He was only about eighteen, probably the same age as the Aboriginal he now had to fight. He was not bad, none of the group were real bad, just bad enough to get themselves into problems wherever they went. They were the type of blokes that my mother dreaded I would end up knocking about with, the type who always had run-ins with the police. But they weren't real bad.

We all marched out of the tent to watch. The crowd formed a circle around the two boys and we waited. One of the old professionals had come with the tent fighter, the same man who had fought our soldier. Fights in the street were pretty fair in those days, if a man was beaten the fight was stopped. Feet, knives or bottles were never used, that would come later. But Pat's mob were not entirely to be trusted so I was happy to see the big old white fighter warning Pat that only fists were to be used, and to the rest of us that nobody was to interfere.

The two boys stripped to the waist, shaped up and moved around each other. Pat held his hands low, he wasn't a boxer, he didn't even look like a street brawler, he was small, but his size was misleading, he was strong, wiry strong, the type of strength that a lot of people can't see, and he didn't give in easily, I had seen him fight many times. Cessnock was a small town.

The Aboriginal boy crashed a straight left, a bare fist into Pat's face that opened a deep gash inside his mouth. Blood-flecked spit bubbles spurted out with every breath he took. The tent fighter stepped quickly away and then moved back even more quickly throwing a left and a right, another straight left and then a left hook. The Aboriginal fighter was a rare man who was born to fight. He could take his ring skills and use them effectively in the street where a mad swinging no-rules contest often left a trained boxer with no great advantage. The Aboriginal boy's timing never faulted against Pat's mad rushes. His power, speed and delight in fighting left Pat defenceless.

Pat was cut high on his forehead, thin steams of blood rushed down his face over the bridge of his nose and mixed with yet more blood streaming from his nostrils and mouth before cascading onto his bare breast, matting his light covering of hairs. He had smeared his face crimson by rubbing the back of his hand across his wounds, one eye was closing and his lips had swollen. His face resembled a richly-painted, grotesque Chinese opera mask. And still he would not quit.

It was Pat's gang that stopped the killing. Two of them wrapped him in an embrace of mate-ship, holding his arms to his sides. Pat didn't resist, he could barely stand. The Aboriginal fighter moved back a step. 'Do you still think we are just black Abo bastards?' he asked in a high excited voice. All Pat answered was that he was beaten fairly, before he turned slowly, and walked away unsteadily.

Pat was one of us, a Cessnock boy, but most of the blokes who had walked out of Sharman's boxing tent were behind the Aboriginal fighter. Probably all of us were guilty of calling an Aboriginal a black Abo bastard at some time, even if it was not to his face, but we also had a pretty fair sense of what was right, and this wasn't.

What bothered us most in those days about the Aboriginals were their bad work habits, their walkabout mentality, the drinking that left them staggering, aggressive drunks. In our eyes they were social misfits who were supported by the taxpayer. But here was a bloke who was a fighter, that was something we could respect, a man having a go, not a falling-down drunk living off the rest of us. It wasn't about colour, it was just about difference, and with this bloke there was no difference. That's the way we liked it.

In 1969 in Cessnock, it did not occur to us that there may have been strong reasons for these differences. We had no sense of their spiritual need to acknowledge the dreamtime, follow the songlines, or as we understood it, 'go walkabout'. We didn't really consider that they would choose to live free and independent from us had they been allowed or encouraged. We were only vaguely aware that the European settlers had dispossessed them of their land, destroyed their communal life, their culture, and that we had left them drowning in an ocean of two unrelated cultures. We just never believed that the Aboriginal way of life had significance and so could not understand why it would be so difficult to leave it behind and embrace ours.

As I wandered back along the alley, dodging the crowd who were not looking where they were walking because the carnival had stolen their hearts, consumed their minds and affected their sense of direction, I came once again to Sharman's boxing tent. The drums had stopped beating and the tent flap had been closed. All that was left to distinguish it as a house where men worked was the mural of our champions that was now dancing intimately with a breeze that had come suddenly and blew gently. I stared up at the painted fighters who were the princes of our world but didn't linger, there was no need, I would see them again next year. I would be sixteen, it would be my turn to have a go.

1969 was the last year that Jimmy Sharman's boxing troupe travelled the fairs around New South Wales. Our politicians decided that same year to ban tent boxing. They thought it unsafe. They had decided, these politicians, that it was their decision when we as free men might take a risk in life.

PIGS

The country around Mungindi is flat and dry. Its red soil turns the texture of custard when the infrequent rains come, but most of the year you are choked by dust lifted on the wind, and beaten down by a fierce heat that creates unsettling images that shiver in the distance.

The main street is in New South Wales, but part of the town lies in Queensland, the Barwon River its dissector. A lonely spot, three hundred miles inland from the coast, it can be reached only by unpaved roads, corrugated and rough.

As it flows through the town the Barwon makes small elegant turns, doubling back to see if its tail is still following. White gum trees loom over its banks as if deciding whether to cross, or wait as always. An old wooden trellis bridge spans the river. It was built high because even this river, like all things, shows its rage at times. Just past the bridge on the Queensland side is an old building. Like most houses in the town it was built of wood. It has a large veranda facing the road. Made low, almost ground level, it has easy access both ways. The writing above the front door tells visitors that it is called Tattersals and that it serves beer, wine and spirits.

*

For as long as I remember, every male member of my family had worked as a coal miner. Now many of the pits in Cessnock, my home town, were closed, the coal worked out, or too deep to mine and still make a profit. My father laboured ten years under the ground, only to lose his job along with two thousand men in the dark days of low coal prices and low demand. He was killed ten days later building a road on top of the ground. My grandfather spent the last ten years of his life coughing and spitting, my uncle never returned to the mines after he was almost buried alive, my cousin lost his best friend in the mines, and one year later his best friend's father. My boxing trainer remembered the pit disaster in the thirties when many, many died. My grandfather fought the police who tried to break the strike. 'It was about working with dignity under the ground,' he told me many years later. The town gave the pit the strong backs, the pit gave us our living and pride. Blackened after their work shifts, the men would ride home four abreast, an army of hard, honest workers. There were twelve picture theatres, then three, and shortly after my seventeenth birthday the last closed its doors. *Love Story* was the last film I remember seeing, it was 1971. Most of the work had finished, I would never go down the mines. I was not disappointed: I had never wanted to spend my life underground. I became a bank clerk.

I had been transferred by my employer, The Bank of New South Wales, to this small rural town to take up the position of teller. A local girl who was infinitely more suited to do the job was already working in the branch, but my bank thought it much more efficient to uproot me from my office in Cessnock, my home town, my dying home town, six hundred miles to the south. I had been in Mungindi a week before I crossed the river for the first time and noticed the old wooden building with the large veranda.

*

Inside the Tattersals Pub it was cool. The large gums that grew along the river shaded the drinkers. On Saturdays the horseshoe-shaped bar was always crowded, full of men who had just worked five hard days: property owners, fencers, horse breakers, shearers, roustabouts and bank clerks. The noise was almost deafening as the mostly shirtless or singlet wearing men stood leaning against the bar, talking and arguing, their wide-brimmed hats fighting for space on the counter with tall ice-cold glasses of beer. The barman moved constantly. He worked alone, his large frame effortlessly pulling new beers and keeping conversation with different men around the bar. His tattoos shimmered like drowned corpses in their bed of hair and glaze of sweat.

In one corner stood a group of Aboriginals dressed only in shorts and rubber sandals. They had walked the five miles from their home on the government mission to drink in a town that barely tolerated them, but that was more than most did. NO WOMEN ALLOWED, read the sign next to the entrance door.

The first punch landed high, forcing rather than knocking the older of the two men back against the wall. By the time I had swivelled on my bar stool to get a better look, another ten punches had landed, the fight was finished. A stocky man in his early twenties with a shock of thick blond hair and a bruised and swelling left eye walked quickly from the bar, the winner. 'What the hell? Don't worry, mate,' comforted the bloke sitting next to me, 'It's just Jack and Ned, almost a bloody ritual, I've seen them fight more times than I've slept with my missus. Ned always wins. He's too young, too fast, too strong, and besides, Jack is always drunk. Funny thing is Jack always manages to damage Ned in some way, and when Ned looks in the mirror he gets so angry, the next time they meet, they fight again. If you ask me, I think they really like each other.'

The walls of the old place, like most pubs I've been to, were covered with photographs. The local football team took up the most space. The boys proudly posing in their maroon and white uniforms, bloodied and defiant. Alongside came photos of racehorses, long muscled animals streaked with white lines of salt and sweat crossing the winning post, or being led by jockeys in tight white riding pants and vibrantly coloured blouses to accept trophies from large ladies wearing large hats. One picture, neither of the football team, nor of racehorses caught my eye. It was a photo of Ferrell, my new drinking mate. We had first spoken when he sat down beside me at ten that morning, pub opening time, and ordered 'a bloody cold one mate, for me head.' His long lean body draped itself comfortably across the bar as he drank. When he talked to you he would often touch your shoulder or forearm, our friendship came easily. In the picture on the wall, Ferrell was smiling broadly, squatting beside a large dead pig, blood staining the wild animal's chest. In his hand he held a knife. Dogs with powerful shoulders and large broad heads worried the dead animal. Ferrell was a pig chaser.

Pigs were vermin, I had been told on numerous occasions since moving to Mungindi. Since their introduction by the English as domestic and hunting stock, they had multiplied. Running wild, breeding rapidly, and with no natural predator they had become a dominant tribe. Travelling in large groups they broke down fences, trampled the wheat crops and savaged new-born lambs. They deserved to die.

After hearing this story so often I was not surprised to learn that pig chasing was the sport of choice for the men of Mungindi. It was also how they judged each other. Nobody could respect you if you had not killed. I was not brave enough not to kill. I realized suddenly and with great apprehension that I would have to kill a pig.

To chase wild pig Mungindi-style you could use only a knife. In theory, trained dogs would hold the pig by the ears, giving you the chance to grab the back legs, throw him onto his back, place your knee under the chin of the struggling animal, secure his front left leg vice-like between your left arm and body, and finally drive your knife down through his throat into his heart. All the while avoiding the sharp tusks that can open you or your dog to the bone, or further.

Sunday was the day chosen. Ferrell said he liked drinking with me, and that meant I would have to chase pigs. But today was Saturday, it was still early and there were many beers still to come, there was plenty of time to feel brave.

It was late afternoon when the horn sounded. Pig time. Ferrell had brought his mate Chock, and five of the biggest, maddest looking dogs I had ever seen. Each wore a studded leather collar for protection against the tusks. They were all excited, ready for the hunt. They knew where we were headed, they lived for this. These were pig dogs.

A wild squeal pierced the air, the dogs could not wait for the chase. They tore at each other madly. Five fighting dogs couldn't be held apart I thought, but then I had only know Ferrell for a day. In he moved, throwing punches at any dog in reach, it was soon over, Ferrell was boss. 'Where do I ride?' I asked after they had settled down, 'In the back with the dogs,' he answered with a large grin. 'You and them are the pig spotters, just don't step on their feet, pig dogs don't like that.'

Through the paddocks we raced, Ferrell's old utility truck bouncing high over every bump on the rough dirt track. Low saltbush scrub covered much of the flat land. The dogs, alert and tense, fought to keep their balance.

The dark shapes in the distance confused me at first, they were moving slowly, unconcerned, relaxed. We had not been spotted.

Without warning they came to life, scattering and moving at speeds that tested the old truck. The shapes were what we were looking for, they were the wild pigs of Mungindi.

Ferrell spun the ute hard and the chase was on. Off the track we turned, speeding towards the group. Forty, fifty miles an hour. We were driving over country made for sheep, one deep hole, one fallen tree stump and we would have been finished, but it seemed that I was the only one to give it a thought.

The dogs were howling wildly, frantically trying to keep the pigs in view as they waited desperately for the truck to slow down. Suddenly Ferrell braked and the dogs were over the side, running hard to the kill. The pigs had split up, the dogs did the same and we followed, sprinting, battling to keep pace, exhausting lungs and legs.

The two pit bull crosses had cornered a large sow. This was my pig. Ignoring the dogs' attack from the side she followed my every movement, turning and twisting to face me as I tried to position myself to take her legs. At last the dogs had her, ripping and tearing at her ears, she was caught, she couldn't move. I took her back legs and with an effort that almost snapped my back threw her to the ground, my knee went to her throat, and I slashed downwards with the knife, missing my aim and opening a deep gash in her stomach. She squealed terribly, I brought the knife back again and plunged it through her throat into her heart. Her blood covered my hands, discoloured my shirt, flecked my face. I stood trembling as she slowly died.

Ferrell and Chock returned roaring with laughter. They were also covered in blood. The result of their carnage scattered over a wide area.

The dog pack was in a frenzy, whimpering with fear and shame. There was still the boar to kill. He waited, ready, furious, but the dogs were afraid. We moved towards the boar together, encouraging, threatening the dogs to stay with us. I looked towards Ferrell and Chock, they were not happy. Like the dogs, like me, they were scared. As we moved closer we could see his dusty matted hair, we could feel his great size, his anger.

With no warning he came at full run, down the hill, head held low, towards us. I turned, all courage gone, and sprinted in the opposite direction. I felt shame, but my fear was stronger. The dogs had retreated and I saw with surprise that my mates, the famous pig killers, were running ahead of me. The paddock was bare, empty except for a tree that had grown old and had fallen, its branches still clinging stubbornly to its trunk. We sprinted behind the leafless cover. The boar came straight on, charging blindly into the branches. It was a mistake. Tangled in the maze of dead wood, unable to use his head, the dogs attacked. The five animals ripped and tore at his trapped body while we slashed and thrust, still too afraid to get close enough for a clean kill, but frenzied by our disgrace at having run. The boar used all his bulk and strength in trying to fight back but he was held by the old dead tree. Except for a few snorts he died silently: boars don't squeal.

I looked towards Ferrell and Chock, at the wildness in their eyes, I listened to their ragged breathing and I hoped that they could not guess how empty and sad I felt.

One of the dogs, a large mastiff bull-terrier cross, had been gored. His throat was split open; his collar had been too small, but according to Chock, who knew about these things, he would live if he was stitched and the bleeding stopped. We left the carcasses to rot, the killing done for the day. Now we would save a life.

Covered in blood and stinking of death we ordered our first beer. Ferrell told our story to anyone who would listen. Baring his uneven teeth he growled ferociously, he had become our dogs, and then he was the boar snorting loudly and swinging his head from side to side, following an imaginary man with his imaginary tusks, and then he was himself, or sometimes Chock, but mostly me. In his story the pigs had become larger, faster, more cunning, the dogs more ferocious, we had become fearless, our cowardice forgotten.

Listening dreamily to Ferrell, I suddenly thought about the Aboriginals I had seen drinking alone in Tattersals the day before. I knew that their ancestors would have told stories of the hunt in much the same way. The exaggeration of bravery would have excited their children, and the children would have learned from the mime, and so the skills of the hunter would be passed on.

And now we hunted and they drank. But we hunted only for the chase, the butchering. We left the meat to waste quickly away under the southern summer sun, stinking and useless, and we told stories for effect.

As I became drunker the remorse faded, Ferrell's exaggerations seemed less exaggerated, my bravery real. It wasn't until the next morning, hung-over and still caked in dried blood, that I remembered.

THE COUNTRY BALL

'When you tap the beer keg be careful. Drive the spear straight and hard through the outer and inner bungs and tighten the lug screw that holds it as quickly as you can. And keep out the way, that bloody keg's got a lot of pressure and if you don't lock in the spear it will shoot straight out and take your head off. I've seen it happen. Connect the hose to the spear, run it to the Temprite spirals, they're filled with CO_2 gas, that'll cool the beer off, and then take the hose to the taps. You're all set. Now mate, when you pull a beer, angle the glass a little, that way it's not all froth. Never pull in one go, three times is the best. And remember, leave a head about two fingers deep, too much head and they'll accuse you of cheating them, too little and the bastards will all yell that it's as flat as a cow turd and refuse to drink it. Keep the glasses rinsed, use a bucket of clean water. But remember, some blokes like to drink from the same glass, the same unrinsed glass. About the women: we've got lemonade, ginger ale, Fanta, Coke, there's Bacardi rum and Bundaberg over-proof rum for the hard drinkers.'

'You know what they say about Bundaberg,' drawled Jimmy from his squat position beside the drinks table where he was smoking contentedly.

'What, Jimmy?' I asked, already knowing the answer.

'If you don't fight when you're drinking Bundaberg then you're really a coward.' Jimmy burst out in a rough, cough-punctuated chuckle. Dave looked down towards him, slowly shook his head, smiled patiently and continued, 'We've got Johnny Walker whisky, Red Label, Jameson's, that's an expensive bastard so don't go spilling it, and try and keep a bit for us at the end of the night, and we've even got Cabernet Sauvignon, although how anybody could drink that stuff is beyond me, but that's cockies for you.'

The breeze had lifted the heat from the brown hard-baked land that was covered in stunted saltbush and carried it along into the night, burning you as it passed. There were no clouds, but in the Queensland Bush there hardly ever were. The stars were thick and white above us, twisting, dancing and stretching from horizon to horizon.

'Get that last keg down from the truck, mate,' Dave called over his shoulder as he walked slowly away towards the darkness at the edge of the light made by the coloured bulbs that had been draped around the woolshed yard; a zigzagging path of delight that ran along the rough wooden fence and over the thick boughs of the thirsty coolibah that stood old and massive, before returning to finish its light circle.

'I've got to take a piss.'

I was a bank clerk, but tonight my work was bartending. Dave, my boss, was a professional barman. He worked days, at the ex-servicemen's club in Mungindi. He had become a barman when his back had given out and he had been forced to stop shearing sheep. Dave was a product of hard, rough work. Tall and wedge-shaped, a stomach like a washboard, longish thick black hair and swollen rough hands that looked too big for the beer taps. He had a badly twisted nose and scar tissue on his lip caused when a sheep swung its bony head into his face while trying to escape the shearing blades. Sometimes this made a smile appear a sneer.

Dave had asked me to work while I stood at the bar of the ex-servicemen's club drinking away the feelings of being a bank Johnny, a clerk in an office that functioned on details and pettiness. I was not good at the first and not comfortable with the second.

'I'll show you what to do, you don't need experience,' he explained to me as he felt my hesitation. 'There'll be the three of us: you, me and Jimmy . . . I got to take Jimmy,' he explained without being asked, 'he's my sister's boy.'

'But what is it exactly?' I asked, dribbling out my words as the alcohol played with my tongue. He smiled, he knew he had me now. 'Macca,' he started, 'it's a great big party with a band, more food than a sty of pigs could eat in a week, all you can drink without drowning . . .'

'And some of the most beautiful young ladies in Australia,' yelled Dennis, the half-Aboriginal, half-Indian bartender, from the other end of the bar where he stood pulling beers for two shirtless, hatless drinkers who were arguing drunkenly, pointlessly, in the back room of the club where the dress rules didn't apply and the air conditioning didn't work.

'Why don't you do the job then?' I yelled back.

'Not me,' he replied, 'you won't finish till the sun comes up. It's a young man's job, I'm getting too old.'

'Look,' continued Dave, 'it's held in a woolshed on a big property in the middle of nowhere, about fifty miles from here. They call them balls, bachelor and spinster balls. It's an excuse for those rich land-owners, the cockies, as we call them up here, to get together and match up their kids, talk about sheep. They get dressed up in smoking. You're gunna have the time of your life, and you get paid.'

*

And here we stood in our white shirts and narrow ties, waiting in the dust; ready.

The band had set up just outside the shed on an elevated platform that had been built that morning. They were five men, four dressed in dark suits and bow ties and the fifth, the singer, the leader, in white. A dark shiny piano carried the rhythm and the man in white, who was not young, sang with a voice that was high and clear. He started with *Frankie and Johnny*, a Jimmy Rodgers song from the thirties. This band was old-time.

My first beers were not the best according to Jimmy, too much head, or too little. Dave just smiled as he listened. 'I got to love him,' he finally said to me, 'he's family.' Then he turned to Jimmy, 'Shut your mouth, all you know about beers is drinking them.'

The dancing had started, it was a foxtrot even though the dancers were young and looked the age when heavy metal rock bands like AC/DC were supposed to move your heart.

Thick brown dust kept pace with the late model cars and pick-ups that drove unendingly through the gates of the property and sped the quarter mile to the sheds. Young men sprang quickly out in order to open the doors for the girls who were dressed in chiffon and lace, taffeta and silk satin.

'Good looking sheilas, eh?' whispered Jimmy, not wanting anybody but me to hear as he pulled a beer for a young man wearing a red bow tie at a crooked angle. 'These people have got it easy, rich bastards, those girls have got nothing to do all day but look good. Look at the clothes, city clothes, expensive as hell. A few years in the university, then they come back and marry their own kind, and that's not our kind mate. More land than anybody needs. Some of these properties are over two hundred thousand acres, and the sheep, Christ mate, there's enough woolly jumpers on this place alone to keep the population of New South Wales warm in the winter.'

The band played a song that my grandfather would have known the words to: a quicker rhythm with a country lilt. A few couples moved together as if they had learned to walk in each other's arms, floating across the boards that had been laid down for the dance, swaying in and out of the other dancers who were skipping and swinging in an inelegant attempt at keeping pace with the music.

Dave pulled me a beer. 'Get that inta ya, mate. Ya doing all right. But listen, don't take too much notice of Jimmy, I overheard what he was telling you. Sure, some of these buggers need pulling down a peg or two, especially the young ones that have never had to battle for anything, but this country up here is hard, saltbush scrub mostly. Where the rivers run you get a better soil, more grass, but there are not many rivers. You've got your bore drains of course, and if you make drainage channels it helps a bit, but you still need a lot of bloody land to keep them sheep happy. They're having a good run now, prices for wool are strong and we've had some good rain, but mate, when they have it hard the banks are waiting to pounce.'

'Yeah,' I replied, 'but the way they dress and talk.'

'Look mate, we've all got our uniform. I don't much like those white moleskins they're always wearing, or those bloody short-sleeved check shirts, but I wear elastic-sided boots just like they do, and a hat, even if it's not the same neat shape. I know some of them talk like their bloody tongues are stuck to the top of their mouth, but not all of them. They stick together mostly, that's for sure, but everybody likes to be amongst his own. That's the way it is. Tomorrow you play cricket against the Boomi club. That whole team's mostly cockies. Oh mate, the women, the wives and girlfriends will lay on a feed for you you won't forget for a long while. And when you finish drinking with those boys after the match you'll see what I mean. I worked for a lot of these men when I was shearing. If you're fair with them, they're all right. You haven't been here that long, Macca. Don't take too much notice of the likes of Jimmy. He's a good bloke, not too bright poor bugger, but he's like most of us in that he tears down anything that grows above him. But that ain't right.'

The band played *Tennessee Waltz*, a song that always reminded me of thick sweet honey. The dancers were pulled close together by the music as they swirled around.

She caught me gazing, staring. Her soft golden hair that darkened in places when she moved in and out of the shadows made by the coloured lights was cut straight, just reaching bare shoulders. Her nose, which turned upwards a little, was slightly freckled, but in a way that showed you it had always been protected by a wide-brimmed hat. She was slight but strong, and the indigo flowers on her silk taffeta dress made her light blue eyes deep and clear.

'You despise us don't you?' she asked, looking at me directly.

'No,' I answered quickly, smiling to hide my embarrassment. But I was not sure . . . As I watched all the young pampered wealth about me eating from tables laid with oven-baked hams and mutton, freshly barbecued beef and pork chops, steaming, boiled potatoes, chickens that had been stuffed, baked, and left to cool before serving, fruits and salads that had travelled from the coast three hundred miles away. Or listened to their conversations about wool prices and the cost of their new machinery, their father's new machinery, or the trips to Sydney eight hundred miles away on their planes to watch a game of cricket, I was not sure. I came from a coal-mining community where nobody got ahead of one another or the rest of the world. But it was more, I knew that I couldn't have her because she was one of them.

'Bastard,' screamed Dave, looking towards the gates at the four cars racing along the track towards the party. They were old cars, dented and dirty. Holden utes, a Ford Falcon, machines that were not loved, only used, misused in rough country by rough boys. And they were moving fast, driving so recklessly, their dust mixing, forming a thick cloud, smothering a corner of the sky. They drove so close together that they blinded each other, but still they didn't slow. They were coming for trouble.

The cars came to a stop at the edge of the darkness in the half-light made by the black night and the electric lights. They didn't squeal their wheels, you can't on dirt, but their cars wiggled and slid, sending small stones and chucking fine dirt into the watching crowd. The doors seemed to open in unison, spilling out young men from both sides of the cars. They came towards the coloured lights. Some staggered and swayed, all looked like they had been drinking. They wore jeans and loose hanging T-shirts. Their arms were covered in rough blood-red and deep-blue tattoos; an unalterable war paint. It was the uniform of a town boy, a drinking boy. It was difficult to see what they looked like, only their movement and madness gave an impression of who they were.

The boys had come from Moree, a town of eight thousand people ninety miles to the south, a wheat town dominated by tall round silos that stored the grain brought in from surrounding districts. Moree was a town where you chose a place to drink a beer carefully. A place where pubs were segregated into black and white, rough and less rough. Moree boys didn't like cockies.

One came striding ahead of the others. Thickly built and needing to fight. When he reached his first young cockie standing amongst a small mixed group that had herded for safety, he brought back his right hand and punched towards the boy's surprised eyes. The cockie threw his right hand up trying to block it and lost his grip on the beer glass that he had been holding, sending it somersaulting into the group, wetting the smokings, the taffeta and lace. Like small grass fires that burst independently into life as offspring of a parent fire blazing away on a hot windy day, fights started throughout the yard. There was no battle ritual, no circling or name calling, no tentative shoves to test the strength, the willingness of the opponent. Straight in they went, fighting till the fight was worn out of them. Some of the cockies fought back, but in a defensive way, never taking advantage of their numbers. Most tried to ignore it, deny it, instead of driving the Moree boys out. Dave turned to me, 'Jim's missing, I got to find the silly bastard before he gets hurt, he don't like cockies too much, but nobody likes these bastards from Moree. Whatever you do don't serve them drinks, and don't let them near the bottles.'

I thought that was a pretty tall order considering the situation, but only once during a lull in the fighting, a sort of in-between rounds, was I asked for a beer by a shirtless Moree fighter with a pig dog tattooed over his right breast and two fingers missing from his left hand, something you only noticed in the stronger light near the bar.

'Not here, mate,' I answered, and he just grunted, turned, and started drinking a half-empty beer that had been left by a cockie, who I assumed needed two hands at that moment.

The fights continued in different places throughout the yard for more than an hour. Not continuously, but in bursts, which were always followed by a period of calm. The Moree boys had spread out and would simply join a group of cockies and when the nature took them wheel in and start throwing punches; or not. By the end of their visit some were even chatting to the young men dressed in smoking, as if they were old friends. The band that had stopped playing when they first arrived now produced waltzes and foxtrots with indifference.

They left quickly and with little fuss. A signal had been given, a word or a whistle. One or two had to be helped to the cars, drunker now than when they arrived, but most looked like invited guests who had to leave early. There was no yelling, no abuse. They had disrupted the ball, left people bleeding and shaken, soiled and humiliated. They had broken lanterns and trampled over the food. The tables that had been decorated so elegantly lay on their backs, their legs extending upwards like drought-dead sheep. But the bar, like a childhood memory, had remained untouched, untainted. Soon the band played unnoticed while everybody gathered around the kegs and the whisky bottles, trying to bring back the gaiety that had been bashed out of the night.

The sun had grown to its full bright yellow roundness. But it was an early maturity, a large puppy sun without real power or fierceness. A cool breeze that belonged to the night still blew about us. We had just loaded our last empty keg onto the ute. The music had finished hours ago, but the bar had stayed open until the last drinker had given up and lay cradled by the tall gum in the empty yard.

'How do you feel, Macca?' asked Dave as he handed me the last mouthful in the last bottle of Jameson's.

'Drunk,' I answered honestly, 'real drunk.'

And so we drove the seventy miles back to Mungindi, or rather Dave, who was less drunk, drove. Jim had passed out before we had loaded the kegs.

'Get up ya silly bastard, ye got to play cricket at Boomi.' It was my landlord big Jack bellowing.

'Bugger off, it's still night time.'

'It's eleven in the morning and you got to drive ninety miles, the game starts at one.'

'Jesus mate, why didn't you wake me?' I complained. 'What about the rest of the team?'

'All gone mate, you've got to head up there alone.'

'Jesus mate, I'm crook.'

'You'll be right, I'll get your car started.'

As I drove through the Sunday-dead streets of Mungindi, racing over the bridge that spanned the Barwon river, past the Tattersals pub with the low roof and large veranda, and deep into the heat-miraged, sheep-infested outback that was Queensland, I opened my first cold one. Just one for the head and heart I thought. My car, a '68 Falcon 500, white and wonderful, hugged the rough, hole-riddled dirt tracks that were thought of as roads in Queensland as if born to outback driving. Sixty, seventy miles an hour, throwing out the rocks, dirt-dusting the stumpy vegetation, frightening the mobs of emus, dodging the roos that bounded startled across the track as you passed, swinging the wheel to squash the snakes that thought they could warm themselves on your road. On we went. Just one more cold one ought to be enough.

The rise in the road didn't frighten me or my Falcon. We took it without slowing, lifting and riding into nothing. Airborne for the slightest of moments, down again. But the road had twisted, trying to shake us off. We twisted with it, but the Falcon lost her balance and began to keel inelegantly, dangerously. I rode her on an angle further and further, her two wheels digging in, gripping the ground, doing her best. But we had taken it too fast, too easy, too drunk: over we went and over again.

I crawled through the front windscreen swearing at my bad luck as only somebody who's lucky to be alive can, and then returned to retrieve my cigarettes that were inside of my upside-down car. My hands began shaking badly as I directed a smoke towards my mouth. The match flame danced jerkily as I held it against my cigarette.

I was still squatting in the middle of the track under the midday sun drawing deeply, trembling, when the utility braked hard beside me.

'Saw that big puff of dust, mate. I knew somebody had tipped her, but you're all right, that's the main thing. You are all right, aren't you mate?

'My name's Jock,' he drawled as we drove up the track that led to his house about a quarter of a mile from my wounded, soon-to-be-pronounced-dead car. His wife opened the door that was screened with fine mesh wire to keep out the flies and without saying anything handed me a steaming mug of sweet black tea. 'You all right,' she then asked, before leading me to the table decorated with a flower-patterned tablecloth and plates of baked potatoes, chicken, pumpkin and green beans. Piles of white bread lay waiting to be buttered and eaten along with the other food. A huge teapot stood in the middle.

The polished iron, wood-burning stove that stretched the length of the back wall spewed out heat which collected under the tin roof already hot from the midday sun. We had come in through the back door, the kitchen door. It had been their feed time, Sunday baked-dinner time when I had crashed. Jock, his wife and his three teenage daughters had been eating.

Jock radioed the Mungindi police, Queensland side. He spoke to Dicky Brandon. Brando out of uniform, never Dicky. Sergeant Brandon when working. Everybody knew him: it was a one-man police force Queensland side.

'You've got to have a police report for the insurance,' Jock explained to me, 'and don't worry about the beer cans, they're in the back of the ute. Can't have him thinking you were drunk. Anyway, it's Sunday lunch, he's probably drunk himself by now.'

While we waited for Sergeant Brandon we ate and Jock told me about his twelve thousand acres. 'It's a small property out here mate, got some wheat planted, run some sheep, but it's bloody hard making the ends meet. Too small really,' he said to the piece of chicken impaled neatly on his fork. 'It's a dead country when there's no rain, a sad country, and I can't afford help. Lucky I got me missus and the girls. The two youngest use the radio for their schooling. June, she's the eldest,' he continued, pointing at the tallest of the girls with his now empty fork, 'she's normally away at uni, but when she's back she pitches in too. Man's lucky when he got a family like that.'

I was only half listening; June and her sisters took the rest of my attention.

Sergeant Brandon arrived about an hour after the crash dressed in Sunday civilian clothes. He was wearing snug-fitting bottle-green shorts that seemed to be strangling his huge thighs, balls and arse, and squeezing the blood from his waist. His large hairy belly was left bare by a too-tight short-sleeved check shirt that stretched over his broad back and shoulders but failed to reach down past his belly button. He wore his riding boots sockless, and just to show that he was working, finished off his outfit with a blue-and-white check police cap tipped high back on his forehead.

'What are we supposed to call you today?' asked Jock smirking, 'Brando or Sergeant Brandon?'

'Call me what you like, Jock, just don't smile when you do it.

'What the fuck happened to you, Macca? You all right?'

It took five minutes for Sergeant Brandon to satisfy himself that the Falcon was indeed crashed and that there were no suspicious circumstances, only stupidity. 'Macca,' he growled to me, speaking past a burning cigarette that hung from his mouth, 'come to the station tomorrow and we'll get the details, it's too bloody hot here. Now piss off to the cricket.'

'How do I do that, Sergeant Brandon?' I asked through the smoke of my own cigarette.

'Ah fuck, get in the car. I'll drive ya. It's the life of a poor bloody bush copper. How far is it?' he asked while sliding his huge body behind the wheel.

'Another thirty miles,' I reckon.

'Shit,' he quietly replied.

As we neared the oval at the edge of the town Sergeant Brandon switched on his siren. Its wailing caused the bowler to stop mid-run, the batsmen and fielders to turn and look. The onlookers to wake from slumber and the children to squeal with delight.

'I brought Macca,' he yelled out of the window to no one in particular as he skidded to a stop. 'Sorry mate,' he said turning to me giggling, a giggle that sucked the air back into his throat and made strange sounds, one that made his belly rise up and down. 'This place don't have much excitement.'

'Put the pads on, Macca, you're in next.'

'What's the score?'

'We're eight for a hundred and twenty. Get some runs, mate.'

I could bat a bit, but who couldn't. Normally I would open, but due to the delay I was coming in at number eight, the tail end. The field was placed for tail-enders and the bowlers were confident.

The ground was packed red dirt, grassless: a strawberry-coloured moonscape. And it was fast. As I took centre I noticed for the first time that the pitch was made of matting, a bush innovation where water was too precious to waste trying to grow grass. As I looked around, surveying the field placings, I had the time to see just how lonely a ground I was in. Flat scrub-smothered emptiness. Behind the bowler stood the town that included a small general shop, three or four weatherboard houses, one had been painted a light pink colour but that had been many years before, and a pub that leaned ever so slightly. A Four X beer and a Balimba sign hung either side of the front door. Its name was painted in large white letters just under its wrought-iron balcony, but I couldn't read it. A towering wheat silo stood just past the last house. Boomi was a wheat town. On my hooking, pulling side, stood a massive tree with branches that stretched outwards and upwards forming a shady canopy of leaves. Under the tree stood supporters, interested onlookers, children and dogs. Just behind it limped two hobbled horses sniffing sadly at the red dirt. Cars and utes, colourless under their dust blankets, lined the road running past the tree and through the town.

A silly mid-on and a silly mid-off stood almost within reach of my bat, two slips, a gully, third man and a fine leg fanned out from the wicket behind me, a mid-off and a mid-on halfway to the boundary finished their trap.

A bowler dressed in the impeccable white uniform of the fair-dinkum cricketer came pounding down through the soft dust intent on taking my head off. But I was waiting, ready.

I cut, hooked, pulled and drove, and often I snicked, all with the madness of a man who has survived a bush car crash. The fours came easily on the small ground of hard-packed dirt. Boomi moved the fielders in, out and around. They changed bowlers, speedsters, medium pacers, spin, but fearlessness brings its own luck, and by the time they had bowled out Peto, our last man, who only played because as he had so often told us, 'It gives me the chance to get the hell away from me missus for the day and get pissed,' I had made sixty-two not out. We were dismissed for one hundred and ninety-five: a terrific score in the bush.

As is country custom, the small crowd applauded as we left the field. Peto, who had been bowled for a duck on his second ball, dragged his bat left-handed through the dust as if his time at the crease had exhausted him, and, with his right hand laid horizontally across his stomach, bowed left and right, and left again.

A table had been set up under the old tree and laid with a spotless red check tablecloth. Women in sleeveless cotton dresses stood around the table armed with tea towels, whipping at the air, hunting the black flies that were thick and hungry. All the ladies wore wide-brimmed hats, mostly made of straw; one or two wore bush felt hats, rough and bent out of shape. On the table lay platters of meat: boiled ham, oven-fried chicken, mutton. Sandwiches, salads and homemade bread and butter were placed at intervals. Jam and fruitcake had been prepared.

As I squatted to unbuckle my pads, John our captain, who was only thirty-two but whose grey hair and perpetually worried face made him seem a decade older, dropped his heavy frame down beside me and handed me a cup of sweet black tea. 'You all right Macca?' he asked quietly.

'Quite a spread they've laid on,' I answered. A smile came to his face and then he began to tell me how renowned the Boomi women were for their tables. 'They're all cockies, or rather wives, sisters and mothers of cockies. Jesus they can cook. Every year I look forward to playing here.'

As I slowly sipped the too hot tea, I took time to gaze at the life going on under the tree. The women, some of whom were quite beautiful, skipped around the table, cutting the meat, serving the cakes, pouring the teas, killing the flies, smiling, chatting and flirting. Our boys, to my surprise, were not grouped together but sprinkled among the Boomi boys. They talked loudly between mouthfuls of food.

'I thought they would be different,' I finally said to John who was still squatting beside me. He just gazed and smiled, not understanding. John pulled a packet of Winfields out of his shirt pocket, slid out a cigarette, and before lighting up used it to point towards a group of men standing at the end of the table where the last pieces of fruit cake were being served up. 'See that bloke over there,' his worried look had returned, 'that's Robert Conrad, and see that other one, that big-shouldered, healthy-looking bastard with the mouthful of food, that's Peter Conrad. They're brothers and they're terrific. Last year they hit everything we bowled at them. Macca, it was terrible. I cramped in the leg muscles from chasing the ball. They had to stretch them back over my head to ease the pain. I looked like a crab turned on his back. That's no way for a captain to look.' John said nothing for a moment, and then turned his face upwards towards the sun as if trying to burn away the memory . . . 'Anyway,' he continued, 'the point I'm trying to make is, if we don't watch them today, they're going to knock us to hell and back. Again.'

Robert Conrad sent the second ball straight back over the head of the opening bowler for six, but the third ball skidded on a piece of frayed matting and flew off the inside edge of his bat as he tried to lift it for another six. It snapped his leg stump into two pieces. Robert Conrad had no respect for our bowling. His brother, who also had no respect, made thirty-one runs in nine minutes before he hooked a ball high towards third man. In most cases this was a fairly safe shot as Peto always played at third man, and as far as anyone could remember had never caught a ball in his life. But today was a strange day. Peto had only drunk tea during the change of innings and a sober Peto was a safe-hands Peto. He stumbled, wobbled, but took the catch with both hands pulled to the chest like a real cricketer. It took an hour and a half to bowl, catch, and run out the last of the Boomi team. They had scored one hundred and thirty-five. We had fielded during the hottest part of the day, soaked in sweat and smothered in black, salt-licking flies, but we had given our best, and today it was good enough. Now it was pub time.

The old hotel was cool and dark as you entered from the white-hot light. It had a long straight bar that was covered with towels to protect its woodwork from the beer. The walls had been tiled halfway up and all the way around. Exotic beer coasters had been collected and pasted above the tiles.

Tall stools lined the bar, but we quickly shoved them aside to make more room. The cricketers stood shoulder-to-shoulder leaving themselves just enough elbow room to bring their beer glasses to their mouths and back again to their resting places along the bar that was crowded with caps already soggy with spilt beer. Noise echoed in the small room as men told stories that became more untruthful by the mouthful. The women and children stayed together in another room drinking lemonade and shandies: they weren't allowed in the main bar.

I called for another couple of beers from the bartender who had been one of the Boomi cricketers. His white shirt had been replaced by a blue singlet that he wore tucked neatly into his long cream coloured pants. He still wore his peaked cricket cap and studded white boots.

'Rough day, mate?' I turned and saw that it was Robert Conrad.

'Rough weekend,' I answered truthfully.

'Did you go to the ball?' I asked Robert after more beers had washed more cricketing lies about the bar and the laughter had become so infectious that it began to use up drinking time.

'Nope, but I heard about it, and I'm sorry I wasn't there.'

'Why didn't you blokes just drive them out, there were enough of you?'

'What do you mean, "you blokes"?' Robert answered suspiciously.

'Cockies, mate – you blokes.'

'We're not a mob, mate. If the Moree bastards looked like they were on top, it's only because they swung into the wrong cockies. I promise you, if it had been me or my brother or some of the other blokes you played against today, you'd have seen some Moree blood and snot fly.'

By local club rules, the first three beers for each of our players were paid for by the Boomi Cricket Club. But men who had travelled for ninety miles on roads better suited to horse and cart, stood for hours unshaded under a fierce sun to chase a small red ball around a pinkish-dirt oval in the name of recreation, do not leave after three cold delicious beers.

It took the complaining of the children and the constant nagging of the women, theirs and ours, before the mood of mateship was overtaken by feelings of responsibility and remembered vows of commitment, and the men sadly started to leave empty glasses on the bar and wander out into the thick black night.

THE PORNO NIGHT

Wind always seemed to whistle through Joe's nose as he spoke. It was because it had been badly broken, because he had played so many Rugby League games in the front row of scrums where fists, forearms and heads were used against noses.

'Macca, I'm a Roman Catholic. We can't start up this club with money earned from a porno night.' When Joe said this his chest, which was shaped like a small hill, rose and fell. His hands, which resembled fur-handled hammers, opened and closed, and opened again. The six men seated around the table in the back room of Joe Maguire's pub stared at the beers next to their empty note pads and said nothing.

The idea for the porno evening had been Cock's. The reaction from the other committeemen around the table had been enthusiastic. 'People always pay to look at tits and arse, we'll make a plenty of money.' This insight came from Pat, who didn't suffer from his father's moral dilemmas. Pat was also Catholic of course but the Holy Trinity had never had a strong influence on him. Joe had not despaired, but satisfied himself that Pat was a decent man, which he was, and left it at that.

'Real fucking,' whispered Jimmo, a thin-armed, hollow-chested, heavy-drinking regular with a bald head that gave off no reflection, even under the lamp that hung directly above him. He was speaking to himself as he scribbled nippleless breasts on his pad. He didn't realize he was doing it – or that we were watching him.

Only Dougie, our most sober committeeman, pointed out that our plan was illegal, and, he continued, 'for those that are married or attached, there's bound to be trouble.'

'That's all right, we trick the coppers and don't tell the wives.' It was Cock again. Everybody looked around, unsure, searching for confidence in the faces of the other men.

'And what about Joe?' said sober Dougie, still searching out the problems.

'Joe, what if you weren't present at the meeting?' I suggested, giving him the slyest of winks. Joe rose as fast as his large ageing frame allowed, and left carrying his glass. As he reached the door he turned and nodded his head to us, his thick grey-streaked hair fell over his forehead, a large smile creviced his face. 'See youse in the bar,' was all he said.

This was the second meeting held to establish Joe Maguire's Rugby League Club. We hoped to enter a team in the country zone competition that included all the small dead mining communities and rural outposts around the town of Tamworth, my new bank posting, in the New South Wales bush. It was said that this competition lacked flair and beauty, that the pace was ponderous and the skill negligible, but the enthusiasm and spirit were acknowledged, and everybody knew you had to be a hard bastard to play in it. Joe Maguire had been elected as president. Pat, who had not inherited his father's skills in Rugby League, contented himself with the organization of the club and was given the job of treasurer. I became secretary, and not, as some uncharitable louts had joked, because I was the only one in the pub who could read and write. We had three committeemen: Cock, Jimmo, and Dougie. We needed shirts, balls, medical equipment, we had to insure the players, pay the players, we needed cash.

'Agreed, agreed, agreed!' Everybody fell back in their chairs exhausted from the decision, parched from the experience. We all sauntered out to the crowded bar, heads and shoulders thrown back, papers and pens held visibly, as the proud managers of Maguire's Rugby League Football Club.

It was Pat's suggestion that Cock and I handle the details. Cock was pivotal: his cousin Dennis knew the man known as the Porno King – the man who owned the films.

We telephoned the Porno King from Dennis's house, an old unpainted weatherboard building with broken fly screens and a long scarred veranda that had rotted in places allowing grass to grow through. The house had been built on a burnt, treeless, rock-infested hill near the old sheep yards at the edge of town. It stood close to the back entrance of Joe's pub.

Dennis was mates with the Porno King – he had worked with him years before at The Cross in Sydney. He would handle the negotiations. He did so from his enormously padded, beige-coloured, broken-springed chair that stood in front of his twenty-four-inch black-and-white television. He only left this chair when he needed to fetch cold beers out of the fridge or use the toilet. (When his wife was at home, he left it only to use the toilet.)

The Porno King was a tough negotiator. Cock and I sat beside the chair next to the phone, straining to hear, offering Dennis advice and encouragement. A deal was done, three hundred dollars for a night of filth plus travelling expenses. It would come to three hundred and fifty dollars. Dennis laid the phone back into its cradle, fell back into a relaxed non-negotiating position, looked to both of us for approval, swallowed some beer and burped loudly. We sat fretting: it was a lot of money, a big risk for the club.

We had agreed with the Porno King that he would arrive in ten days. Before that, tickets had to be printed and sold, and we still had to find a secret location to show the films.

Rugby Union and Rugby League started out as the same game almost a hundred years before in England. It began as a manly pastime for the upper and middle classes but soon became popular with the strong-shouldered men that came out of the pits, foundries and factories of Wales and Northern England. The split came in 1895 because of a conflict over money. and because the mixing of classes always left something under-blended: lumpy and unpalatable. The wage-earning workingmen wanted to be compensated for playing on a Saturday, a normal working day in the nineteenth century, but the men who still controlled the game from their dull, wretchedly exclusive clubs in London refused. It was an amateur sport, they cried: 'play the game for love'. But love didn't feed families. The North formed their own governing body, made new rules. It became two different codes.

The Rugby Union boys came to us. They did it through my colleague, Noddy, who was one of the other three tellers at the Bank of New South Wales. Noddy had pale blue eyes, a clear mid-winter's-day blue. You always noticed them. Noddy drank too much as did a lot of lonely bank tellers forced to move from branch to branch by the bank. He was not good with girls and a non-participant in games, but he would drink with anybody and care for who he was drinking with, and this made him welcome wherever he went. Sometimes he drank in the lounges of the better hotels where ladies were permitted and Rugby Union players drank. It was in the Central, a sprawling two-storey white-tiled hotel that stretched itself comfortably around a corner in the heart of Tamworth, that Noddy let slip our plans for organizing a porno night to the Rugby Union set. They too needed to raise money for their club.

We met John McDougal and James Rigby – Rugby Union boys – in the back room of Joe's. They were robust sun-red men who wore the property-owning uniform of check shirt, white moleskins and elastic-sided riding boots. In Australia, Rugby Union was played only in expensive private schools. Rugby League remained exclusively a workers' game. The two codes lived next to each other suspiciously.

I was expecting patronizing aloofness. I was prepared. I came to the meeting with the full sense of being the son of a coal miner, my chip – my coal chip – on my shoulder. Let them try and knock it off. But, I found them only charming, easy-going, eager.

When I thought about it later – five beers later – I realized that Australia in the twentieth century had little in common with the harsh, brutal world of industrial England. Maguire's was a long way from the wet, dark, dust-filled pits of Yorkshire and Wales, or the furnace-heated swelter in the foundries of Lancashire. And our cockies were certainly not to be compared with the old school tie boys that ran their game in England. But historical distaste often sits on your tongue poisoning good food. You have to spit before you eat. We agreed to a partnership over sincere handshakes, pats on the back and extra beers. We would share the risk and the profit, and they would supply a location: we could use an old shearing shed high in the New England mountains. It belonged to one of their uncles. We printed two hundred and fifty light-blue tickets with NIGHT AT THE OPERA black-inked clearly on the front. The price was ten dollars. We sold them in three days. Along with each ticket sold, directions were given to a location on the edge of town where further instructions would be given.

The Porno King arrived on the afternoon of the big night. We stood on the veranda watching him drive into Dennis's yard. His old white Ford Falcon station wagon was covered in mud and rusted around the doors. It had trouble making the hill.

I had been expecting someone powerful, rough even, but when he got out of the car he stood barely higher than the roof. He wore a sagging dark-blue suit that was worn shiny around the backside and elbows, an un-ironed white shirt, no tie, a brown hat with a small rim and black band and when he took it off his jet black hair was slicked tight to his head. His thin moustache left a bare space between his lip and nose. He shook hands delicately, wetly.

The Porno King who, we learned from Dennis, was also called Mouse, was late. Dennis quickly handed out cold tinnies that we drank sitting on his new lounge – still covered in the store plastic, still unpaid for – which stood next to his old chair. Mouse and Dennis huddled together embracing memories of the good old days. Time was running out.

Two Rugby Union players were in charge of getting Mouse up the mountain. The Maguire's boys would take care of directing the punters to the shed and of tricking the police. We sent Mad Nicky (Nicky would sometimes drink his beer at Maguire's standing on his head) and Spud to a junction on the edge of town. Their job was to check out the ticket holders and send them up the frozen winter hills towards the Moonbi Range thirty miles away. 'Look for a big old snow gum just after the road turns back on itself, there'll be a blue Falcon parked on the edge.'

Cock had parked his car close to a drop that fell sharply into a deep fern-carpeted gorge. Across the road, rising up behind the snow gum, was a steep granite cliff that was the face of a bouncing plateau of Antarctic beeches. It had rained in the afternoon and water from a flooded creek spewed down between rocky crevices, splashing across the road and down into the gorge, drowning in the sea of ferns. We sat smoking, waiting for the customers.

Five kilometres further was the gate that opened onto an old track that led through paddocks to a wooden building which, because of the cloaking winter fog, was only visible from one hundred metres away.

The old shearing shed had in the past been used for local dances and bush parties. Rough wooden benches, splinter-dangerous, lined the walls. These we placed as seating in the middle of the hall to face the screen that Mouse had set up against the back wall. Punters who didn't fit on the benches lay on the floor, stood, or squatted, backs pressed into the wall. In the bone-snapping cold of the New England night, we sipped at beer, nipped whisky, guzzled port, waiting for the girls, anticipating the fucking.

The red Walt generator coughed now and again. It could have been a blocked line, or bad fuel, or because it was old and mistreated, but it powered the projector and fuelled the bare bulbs that hung from the rafters, lighting the shed.

The first images splashed onto the screen, a roar filled the hall, obscenities were screeched from all corners.

There was no sound with the films. Mouse's solution was to play popular tunes on a record player, tunes that seemed to match the rhythm of fucking, the mood of passion. We sat through the night, coats pulled high against the cold, swilling alcohol, singing madly – *The Carnival is Over*, *Georgie Girl*, *Yellow Submarine*, *California Girls*, *Angie* – while young men and women groped, licked, caressed and penetrated. On hands and knees, above, below, behind.

Mouse had just announced the end of the programme when Harold stood unsteadily, screaming, 'I want to see a monkey fuck a dog.' Harold was a powerful New Zealand Maori, a Maguire's drinker, a Rugby League player but not one of ours – he played for another club. When he screeched his demand towards Mouse his lips pulled back over his teeth, his broad face became fierce, the

51

spider tattooed on his neck began to crawl over the veins. Mouse's eyes grew with fear. But I could tell by the way Harold's tongue lay heavily on his bottom lip, the deep-red colour of his eyes against his smooth coffee-coloured skin, the way saliva dribbled out of his mouth, that he was just drunk, real drunk, not dangerous. Besides, Harold was a sweet man, we all knew that, everybody except Mouse.

The Porno King scrambled through his collection and quickly put a reel onto the projector. Alpine scenery flickered onto the white screen. A farmyard came into focus. A pretty blonde girl lifted her skirt, tugged down her white panties and was mounted firstly by an anxious German Shepherd, and later by a large pink boar with a corkscrew shaped penis. A narrow-shouldered, thin-nosed, bald man entered the scene, looked disapprovingly towards the woman and the pig (who continued their copulation without taking any notice) and then lowered his pants, spit wet his small hard penis and entered an undersized sow from behind. We all sang *Raindrops Keep Falling on my Head* as loudly as we could, rocking from side to side, howling with laughter.

The night had been a financial and social success. The two rugby codes had got on well. We all drove back to Tamworth as carefully as our youth and the alcohol allowed. The road which was winding and icy, played with our cars, spinning and sliding them. The thick fog in the upper part of the Moonbies challenged our vision and perception. The steep drop on the left side of the road loomed.

My new girl, Jenny, hadn't wanted me to go to the porno night. We had only known each other ten days, but already she had made it clear that anything to do with Maguire's, and certainly with other women, even celluloid ones, would not be tolerated. Jenny was small and strong-willed. She wore her red hair cropped short. A frame for a pale pretty face. At eighteen she was four years younger than me and still a virgin, something I was trying desperately to change. But things were not working out. I was too big she said, although nobody else had ever complained. She was nervous, there were people in the next room, it was the wrong time of the month. I suspected Jenny was holding out for sincerity, commitment, but I was not a sincere, committing man. Jenny saw Maguire's as a competitor, worse, a threat.

'It's a rough pub, it's no good, you're always there,' she would tell me, snuggling close to me wearing only lemon-coloured satin panties, rubbing her small perfect breasts against my chest, caressing my ear lightly with a pointed tongue, tempting me to desert. And I would agree because I desperately wanted to be inside her, and as I have said, I was not a sincere man. Besides, I knew it was impossible to make her understand that Maguire's meant everything to me. That the pub had become my home, the drinkers my family.

At the Bank of New South Wales, I was suffocating in an atmosphere of bickering and misused power. Living a life polluted with rules and conduct. Doing a job that demanded character alignment. There was no room for individuals among the figure-adding staff of yes-men.

'Maguire's is not a suitable place to find one of our staff drinking in,' I was once told by our accountant. 'Drink with us.'

But I found it completely suitable at Joe's. When I stood at the long bar, it was with men who made an honest living without pretensions, whose judgement of you was based no deeper than your willingness to pay your shout, and not try to stand above anybody else.

Joe's was not all harmony of course, not all mateship and good humour. It could sometimes be hard, rough. It was not unusual to see a scuffle. Beer glasses could come crashing down, a chair could fall, a fist would fly, but Joe was quickly around the bar, or over it, his big hair and tattooed forearms driving between arguers, prying them apart. And because he was Joe Maguire the scuffles always ended quickly. And if Joe needed help there was always the rest of the pub behind him. But that was seldom necessary.

At Maguire's, two middle-aged men lived quietly in the rooms upstairs, together. One lean and sad, the other plump and wary. Every evening they would drink downstairs at the bar and we would drink with them, tolerating them, and when, as is usual at times in country towns anywhere in the world, we would sit in judgement, Joe reminded us quickly, firmly, that we were not fit to judge.

Aborigines drank at Joe's because everybody was welcome as long they behaved. And Joe never expected you to behave perfectly.

Sitting on a bar stool, sharing a few drinks with mates you trust and respect in a pub you know and knows you, was as close as I came to being perfectly happy back then. And so I was often at Joe Maguire's.

As you drive into Manilla, both sides of the road are lined by fine old silky oaks as if the town of two thousand people, aware of its small size and isolated setting, wished to provide a guard of honour to anyone who entered. One that they would not quickly forget.

It had rained hard all night, and had eased only a little. This was our first game of the season, our first as the Maguire's Rugby League Club. Manilla was a tough team.

Mud covered the floor of the tin dressing shed. It fell from our boots, tumbling in lumps from our hair, shirts, shorts and faces. New dry shirts had been given out, the used ones lay on the floor, red-flecked, brown-stained.

Blood ran from Sidney's eye wound. It had happened early in the game, but the mud had smothered it, now it ran freely again.

'Why the hell didn't you flatten him, Sidney?' we wondered collectively. But Sidney was our enigma. The scourge of Tamworth street brawlers of whom there were many. A man sent to the city to fight professionally and sent back because he was too wild to handle. He was the iron tip to our wooden shaft but we couldn't get him to throw a punch on a football field. And they were destroying us.

'It's a game, got to play fair,' he drawled. And we knew we couldn't make him. You couldn't make Sidney do anything once he had it in his head not to.

Paddy Wyborn's curly blond hair had turned dark and filthy slick, his head lolled back against the wall, his nose had been broken. He was listening to instructions for the second half. Nippy Johnson our winger had cracked a collarbone. He was the quickest man on the field but now he was finished.

Our coach, wrapped warmly in a sheepskin coat, hands hid deeply in his pockets, told us it was time to reach for some Maguire's fight. 'Tackle hard, run straight.' But it was easy to talk about fighting when you were warm and had no one to fight. We struggled to our feet and slowly jostled through the doorway that was crowded with shivering, wounded Rugby League players who would rather be doing something else. The score was nine nil in their favour. But now, in the second half, we had the wind at our backs.

We were still getting knocked down by their men who hit us in threes. One underneath, two taking our chest and head. In the scrums their big front rowers were scratching, punching and kicking, tearing at our shirts, tugging at our hair, but we fought on, moving the slippery ball around in our forwards, spinning it out to our backs.

Swanny, our nuggetty lock, had been standing at the back of the forwards when Sidney made a run, broke a tackle, turned looking for support, and then passed the ball that had taken on the texture of a mud-covered pig. Swanny took it in full flight, chest high, held on, crashed into three Manilla forwards, and immediately stopped hard. The three men lifted Swanny high into the air, face down.

'Break the mongrel's back,' somebody screamed as he was hurled to the ground.

Water-churned dirt has some spring. It also has less resistance than a dry surface. It allows you to skid. He came down without snapping, slipping a yard or two from the landing. A roar went up from our three carloads of supporters cowering from the weather in their misting automobiles. Swanny had been tossed over the line. He had scored.

'Thanks mate,' I heard Swanny yell to a Manilla bloke through yelps of laughter.

'Piss off ya mongrel,' was the answer that came quickly back. The kick for the extra two points bounded off an upright and plomped over the bar and into the mud like a rock dropped into a sandpit. Two more points. It was nine–five.

My hand began to swell. I had just thrown a right cross at a front row forward, a bullock-chested local farmer nicknamed Simmo. He had lifted up Albert, our wispy Aboriginal halfback who was built like burnt sticks pasted together. He had him locked under one arm and was banging his head with his free fist. I ran fifteen yards to throw the punch, but because of the uneven footing, the slipperiness, my caution for Simmo, I missed his large spread nose and caught him high on the forehead. The punch slid off his skull into nothing. But it was enough, Albert dropped from Simmo's grip and fell like a sack of potatoes, banging into the ground. My punch had only stunned Simmo who wheeled around annoyed, sighted on me, shook his head, turned and joined in the play. And I, still wondering that I had been left untouched, picked up Albert who was crawling around on his hands and knees unaware, like a blind dog sniffing for food. The game thumped on around us.

There were only five minutes left. We had splashed into each other, slid off, pirouetted around, dropped balls, missed tackles, and the rain poured down. Our left winger, Dodger, had pounced on a loose pass and started a sprint towards their line. We all sloshed after him, the dogs after the rabbit. Dodger was fast but alas not our bravest. As the opposing fullback crossed to meet him, Dodger angled away towards the edge of the field until he had nowhere to go and was crashed into the ground over the sideline.

The packs fell together. The scrum was won. Albert sent a diving pass towards me, I flipped the ball out to Cock who turned it sweetly back inside to Paddy the harvester driver who was built low to ground and strong. He busted a tackle, two tackles heading for the line like a derailed train. He fell head first, sliding, his chin making a weak rut in the slush, his broken nose still dribbling snot and blood. A try. It was nine–eight.

Somebody had kicked me in the back, it had happened after I had passed the ball to Cock, as I lay on the ground unprotected. I couldn't move, I thought I would never move again.

Mick the fullback lined up the kick. It was not difficult, ten yards to the right of the post but the ball was heavy. He walked slowly back, ran towards the ball, brought his boot back and down. A large piece of ground flew ponderously into the air somersaulting as it came back to earth. The ball skidded away to the right, sliding a few yards before stopping dead.

'Ya bloody great ponce, Mick,' somebody yelled from the sidelines. We had lost nine–eight.

I was still being worked on as the teams left the field. They glanced as they passed, some enquired about my health, but it was raining, nobody lingered. Our coach sprayed something that was stinging and cold onto my back. His stinking woollen coat was getting soggy. Five minutes later I hobbled towards the dressing shed.

As I entered through the old wooden door that had fallen from one hinge, I saw vapour rising from wet shivering bodies that had warmed in the small, man-filled space. Exhaustion that made tending to wounds, loosening boots, tugging off shirts a demanding task, had overtaken everybody. I flopped down next to Albert who opened a can of Toohey's New and handed it to me. I sipped gratefully, too tired to shower, to hold my head erect, to look forward. Lighting a cigarette, shaking from the effort, drawing deeply, I asked Albert what he had done to Simmo that had made him so mad. Albert gave me a sly grin, closed his fist on his right hand and squeezed. Got him by the goolies, I crushed them big balls of his till he squealed like a sow, like two sows. He then felt his face that had swollen along all of one side, 'Pretty stupid, eh?'

I looked at my own hand that was twice its normal size. 'Yeah,' I answered, 'Pretty stupid. Let's go and have a drink with the bastards.'

On a word, all of our players scooped up full cans of beer and wandered into the other half of the dressing shed – the Manilla half – all animosity forgotten as it always was after a game. Many were stripped, showering, their filthy socks, boots and shirts littering the concrete floor. It was clear they had their wounded as well, but sadly, not nearly as many as us. Simmo ambled towards me and threw a big arm around my shoulders in condolence.

'Why didn't you get into me after I hooked you?' I asked, not knowing what to expect, but confident enough in the post-game tradition of forgiveness.

'Was it you, mate?' he answered frowning, touching a lump that had sprung out of his forehead. 'I can't see too good close up, I'm long-sighted, you were just a blur. You must have been just out of range, ya lucky bastard. Have another beer.'

There are two doors leading to Maguire's main bar. One opens onto the road running past the front of the pub, and the other, a side door, stands just before the pool table, almost opposite the old dartboard. It leads to a large, breezy beer garden. The garden is covered by an old tin roof that because of rusting and popping nails leaks when it rains. The floor is concrete, but over the years it has cracked in places. Peeling, white iron tables and chairs dot the large space like sheep in a drought-dry paddock. A battered old jukebox that plays sad country tunes stands against the wall beside the door. Women are welcome.

A dance was being held in the beer garden when we arrived back at Maguire's. The place was full and loud. Beer was pouring through the hoses, gushing from the taps, filling the tall iced glasses. Joe and Pat were serving from one end of the long straight bar to the other, quickly filling the calico bags that they used in place of a till with worn dollar bills.

At Joe's it was always country music. Tonight it was the Opals, an Aboriginal band from out bush. Six men, all wearing wide white smiles, dusty cattle boots and western shirts embellished with needlework and adorned with fake pearl buttons. Black cowboy hats covered uncut hair that smothered ears. They strummed guitars that had been lovingly used and scarred. And we sang along to the tunes and danced with their women who would pull us barefoot and giggling out of the metal chairs and drag us into the music that lifted and spun us like a floating carousel. Their floral dresses swirled and skipped and the boys in the band were happy for their joy.

After the dance, after drunkenness was complete, after we had helped Joe clear and he had bought us all a last beer for 'doing our best and having a bloody good go against Manilla, because that was the main thing', I left to spend the night with Jenny in her small, cluttered, airless, sweet-smelling flat decorated in frills and pink. She didn't seem to mind that I was late or even that I was drunk. She helped me undress and held me until my stories had faded into sleep.

It was in the uncertain hours when for some, anxieties grip and courage falters. I woke with Jenny lying across me whispering so softly that I could not make out what she was saying.

'What?' I kept asking groggily, 'what?' Licking my dry mouth, tasting only old cigarette smoke and beer.

'I'm ready.'

I finally understood.

'I'm ready.'

I tugged at her panties. She lightly raised her hips until they could slide easily over her bottom, along her thighs and down to her feet where she kicked them into the darkness between the sheets. I gently rolled her off me and began to reach over her, taking the position of a man. I groaned loudly, tried again, and fell back to a flat position on the bed next to her, exhausted and crippled. The kick in the back had not bothered me when it was warm, but during the night my body had twisted into a shape that it refused to bend from. I was useless.

Jenny and I stopped seeing each other shortly after the Manilla game. She was still a virgin.

THE BULLS

The trouble started like most does under a full sun, in a heat that brings simmering blood to a boil. We could hear the teargas canisters tearing into the sky. The dull thud of rubber bullets as they flew from the guns. But we had no idea what they were then. We thought nothing of it. We were Australians, nobody shot at each other where we came from.

We heard later that the trouble began in the bullring. After the bulls and the runners had entered, after the taunting of the bulls had commenced: the pulling of tails, the dancing in front of horns, the pirouetting around danger.

Protestors demanding a free Basque state had paraded banners among the angered bulls and under the gaze of intolerant soldiers. The soldiers must have been expecting something: there were too many stationed around the ring in uniforms already faded by many years of waiting in harsh light for trouble. When violence is organized it spreads quickly. By late morning the fences that kept the bulls running along their corridor from the Santo Domingo corrals through the old city to the ring had been pulled down. Later that day we heard the explosion. It was a bank. And still later another explosion. Another building had been destroyed. Real bullets were now being used. People were wounded and killed. And there we sat amongst our vans and tents beside the towering town wall wondering at the madness. Confused by hatred that was too old for us to understand.

Darrel and I had arrived in Pamplona for the fiesta of San Fermin three days before the rioting began. We drove into a town that had spread downwards through the hills to the edge of the plain in blemishes of ugly, cheap, roughly-built apartment blocks; but after crossing a river and climbing steadily towards the old city it began changing into buildings of thick, solid, cool, unbreakable stone. Shuttered doors led to small flower-painted balconies, that looked out onto cobblestone streets, red-tiled roofs and further to the mountains beyond.

We were directed by an old man with a thick, twisted moustache and a face that had been lined by age and laughter to a camp ground in an area which must once have been a moat. Volkswagen Combi vans, Ford Transits, small buses and cars of all descriptions were parked throughout the space like horses grazing after a long trip. Tents had been pegged out between the cars and vans. Washing hung between tree branches. Cooking fires flickered. Pots and pans lay soiled in the dirt. As we drove through the community looking for a place for our own Ford Transit, Bob Dylan sang *Joey* to us from a rusting green Combi, Linda Ronstadt serenaded us from the opening of a small two-man tent. Steely Dan and The Eagles battled for an audience in another part of the camp. Shirtless, deeply-tanned men who still wore their hair a little long sat in groups in the dirt with women who stayed cool by wearing very little. They were drinking, laughing, touching. Some strummed guitars, some each other. Still others wandered aimlessly amongst the vans and tents, looking, searching for action. We could hear the accents of other Australians, New Zealanders, white Africans, British, Irish. Languages from

Northern Europe jousted with the English. An American dressed in a white shirt, white pants, and a red beret directed us to a free spot near a thick-limbed tree.

'What's the idiot dressed like a cricketer for?' asked Darrel, who was driving and didn't like to be directed anywhere by anybody.

'He's read Hemingway,' answered a skinny, straggly-haired man who had poked his head through our window and offered his wine pouch. Darrel reached across me, grabbed at the pouch and mumbled a thanks before asking in a voice loud enough for the American to hear, 'And who the fuck's Hemingway?' glaring at the American as he motioned us closer to the tree, not wanting an answer from the stranger, and not moving closer to the tree.

Our van was old, blue and rusty, in a way that made you think of an ageing hippie. It had been fitted with a sink, a small gas cooker and a bed. It had already carried us steadily through most of Europe. When we bought it in front of Australia House in London we were told it had been around the continent four times. It had carried people like us who had felt an urge to see something before they settled back to a life of unchanging isolation. Many of us had made no preparation for our trip. We knew little about what had passed our windows as we raced around the continent. We recognized only that the foods were strange and the languages impossible. We thought the architecture overdone, and the arts incomprehensible. For us it was an exotic setting for an endless party. But our nature was easy-going, and our intentions never bad. People who met us and drank with us remembered. And we remembered them.

But sometimes our ignorance led us into areas of ageless discontent and revolt. And here we were in Pamplona amongst unhappy Basques, completely unaware that they had been waging an armed independence struggle for fifteen years.

*

July in the northern Spanish mountains is always warm, and each morning the sun would burn us out of the van and force us to look for the shade of the town built on top of the hill. We would walk slowly because we had drunk too much wine the night before, and because the old stone road that we climbed was uneven and steep. When we reached the Central Plaza Del Castillo we would always go to the same cafe. The one with the shaded terrace, the black and white diamond floor and the small harried waiter who looked like a proud undersized bull, shoulders thrown back, jaw set, pencil ready. Darrel and I would gulp down creamy white coffee and slowly eat sweet *banderilla* cakes, always dunking them first in the coffee. And we would watch the people drift thickly by, bumping and knocking each other like sheep in an overstocked pen. Travellers stumbled and swayed drunkenly. Basques tramped along drinking cheap red wine that they squirted into gaping mouths from leather pouches made for just that. Pretty blonde girls wearing tight cut-off jeans and bright singlet tops danced through the crowd leading a procession of local boys along on a hope. Old dark men wearing black berets sat at tables and watched with bright eyes and knowing smiles, drinking their coffee, saving their strength. Drummers, fife and pipe players marched to the rhythm of their own music through the heat and euphoria.

We spent our time between the town on the mountain and our camp in the moat – between listening to the beat of the drum bands and western rock and roll. People spun around in a haze of wine. Men changed girls and girls men like a shared ice cream you licked some sweetness from and passed along.

Wine and high spirits kept passion tingling. Fights were common. A misunderstanding, an un-meant or meant insult to San Fermin, a social rudeness. The Basques and travellers touched, mixed, but, like chocolate and oil, never blended.

Darrel came from the same coal-mining town as me. His work

as a plumber had left him with a thick rough build, but that was softened by his curly blond hair and by small sky-blue eyes that danced and twinkled. His mouth, which was also small, curled up on one side in an almost perpetual smile. You couldn't push Darrel around, but he would never make trouble. In Pamplona Darrel went a little mad.

People we had met in the moat, who lived in the vans and tents and who came from other parts of the world would tell me to take care of him. 'He's never sober, doesn't wash. He's fighting all the time.' For all his madness, Darrel had made these people worry on his behalf. One night when his exhaustion had forced him home, he slurred his day out to me. 'One fight, one win. These Basques have no tolerance, I was only taking a piss.'

'Where?' I asked.

'In the plaza in front of our cafe,' he answered, howling with laughter. In the morning the heat would wake him early and he would march away on his shoeless black feet to out-drink, outfight the world.

And each morning I would walk the hill to the town and begin my own madness. Through the day and night the girls would pass, linger and move along.

On our third day in Pamplona, the evening before the bulls were to be let loose for the first time, a group of us sat around a fire discussing what running the bulls meant to the Basques, and whether we should run. Wine pouches were passed freely around; tongues loosened.

'It's just a way of proving you've got a working dick,' growled an Australian, who emphasized his point by swinging his wine pouch around his head, spraying us with warm red liquid. 'Where we come from we do it by playing Rugby League or fighting outside the local pub at closing time. There's no need to get a horn up your arse.'

Others talked about the spiritual importance of bull-fighting to the Basques.

'Bullshit,' yelled the same Australian. 'It's about dicks.'

A serious man from Ohio State spoke about Hemingway. Darrel, who had been listening but had said nothing, became ignited by the mention of the name, 'Fucking Hemingway again,' he shouted. But even Darrel said nothing when the young man from Ohio read out a passage. '. . . for the immediate excitement, and it is a very great excitement; and for the retrospective pleasure, of having shown their contempt for death on a hot day in their own town square. Many will go in pride, hoping they will be brave. Many find that they are not brave at all; but at least they went in.' For a few moments all went quiet. Far away a Jimmy Hendrix guitar solo could be heard thrusting and slicing at the night.

'Pretty words like that can get someone killed,' replied the Australian again, 'killed for nothing.'

Some wondered what the fuss was about, they were just here to party. And there were those who thought they should run because there must be nothing more glorious than to show contempt for death. As I did . . . but I was afraid.

I missed the only running of the bulls. I had decided on watching the first day to get the idea, but it started so early and I had been so drunk the night before. I heard the first rocket fired to signal the opening of the pens. And then the second to announce that the bulls had all left. And then I slept again.

The roads out of the city were sealed, there was nowhere to go. We woke to trouble. Barricades had been built to stop the army from controlling all of the city. Cars had been pushed across roads. Tyres burned. Rubble was piled high.

Each evening for the next few days young men still dressed in their white bull running uniform would hurl rocks, bottles and insults. The army was content to wait behind the barricades that were not difficult to push aside and accept the attacks, but on a signal they would fire their teargas, push through, and shoot off their rubber bullets. The crowd would then turn and run like hares chased by hounds. The soldiers would stop, because you can't catch all the hares at night, and return behind the barricades which were only a little damaged. And so it would continue.

During the day Pamplona was deserted and frightened. The empty streets were like dried-out riverbeds, the restaurants empty and sad. Waiters stood unhurried and lost. Soldiers huddled in groups on every corner, guns ready, waiting for the rocks.

In the moat the party went on. The town was too dangerous at night, the war not our war. We stayed with each other. Darrel was still on his good-natured binge, staggering from van to van, fighting if need be. Basques who tired temporarily of throwing things, or who needed protection would run to our camp, certain that the army would not follow them into the international community. They would group around heated and mad, and we would give them alcohol and listen to their stories of Spanish persecution and notions of freedom. At times somebody with a little understanding would point out that their chief persecutor General Franco was dead, that King Juan Carlos seemed like a good, fair man, and that the present government was left-wing and sympathetic to their complaints. But they seemed to find these arguments trivial. 'We want nothing less than an independent state,' they would answer excitedly.

'And the bloodshed?' asked the same man. 'That doesn't bother you?'

'Their blood is not important,' came the reply. 'And we have a lot to give.'

And I thought how exciting it must be for them to be young and have a cause, but I wondered what the idle bullfighters, the cafe and hotel owners, the old people thought. Or the mothers of the dead.

On the second night of the fighting I lay naked in a green two-man tent next to a small, pretty, blonde South African girl with a light sprinkling of freckles around her nose and huge tits that she used as bait to catch someone who could offer her a new life away from her homeland which she thought had only civil war to offer as a future. As she whispered to me in the dark we could hear them fighting in the old city, behind the moat wall. They were using automatic weapons that were loud and threatening and sounded like hail falling on a low tin roof. I got up to put my pants on before I lay down again beside her to sleep. The next day we heard that another boy had been killed.

'Where the fuck is Darrel?' I asked anybody I came across. He had been missing all day and now it was evening. We could hear the battle taking place along a street running beside the moat. The Basque boys had already started to run to our camp to rest and be safe and to accept any adoration that came along. Slowly I moved along the street that was full of the squealing, shouting young men in white shirts and red bandannas. I moved through them searching for Darrel. They moved forward towards the barricades like waves rolling on a beach, retreated, then forward again.

All around me young men hurled objects towards the army on the other side of the barricade. Pretty young women were sprinkled in amongst them, but the violence had contorted their faces, bared their teeth, and made them ugly. I reached the front lines, I could clearly see the soldiers lined next to one another, guns ready. Small tanks were parked behind the soldiers ready to go to work.

When the teargas exploded around us nobody seemed shocked.

Some of the boys raced to collect the gas-spewing canisters and throw them back towards the barricade. They were applauded. Then the tanks, which were small and strong and seemed to have been designed for city fighting, moved forward, crashing through the barricade, rolling the cars and burning tyres away with no more effort than it takes to sweep dust from a house. The soldiers followed, shooting their rubber bullets into the crowd. People tripped over themselves and others as they turned to run.

And I ran: down the road towards the camp, moving shoulder to shoulder with people who had suddenly become my companions. And then back we went again: they went to taunt and wound, and me because I had become part of their game and found it very exciting. It could not have been very different from running the bulls, I thought: people often died at San Fermin. It seemed to me as I looked around that it was not so much about a free Basque state, only that the soldiers had replaced the bulls. Three times I went to the barricades. The second time I was taught how to retreat. 'Left, *hombre*, right, head low, always low.' How to shield myself from the gas. By my third run I had become as confident and as reckless as them.

I found Darrel, wild-haired and black-footed at the end of the street. He was among a group of travellers who were watching the action. He was standing a little bent as if his back had been injured, but I knew it wasn't, he always stood like that. Darrel's hands were slicing the air, wine sprayed from his bottle, he was smiling and spitting. He was telling a story. I could hear the laughter before I reached him. He was safe and happy.

On the third day of the troubles, the authorities cleared the roads and gave us permission to leave. The fiesta of San Fermin was cancelled for the first time in its history. Everybody started packing to the rhythms of rock. Motors started amongst the cries of *adios*. The small South African rode away with a New

Zealander who looked dependable and sincere. Darrel, still unshaven, but freshly washed and sober, drove: he was a far better driver than me.

I hadn't seen a single bull at the fiesta of San Fermin. That first morning while they were still corralled at Santo Domingo and I lay hung-over and safe in my Ford Transit, I had imagined that I could smell the animals whose bodies had been heated and whose minds had gone wild. But perhaps the stench hadn't come from the bulls.

LONDON DAYS

It was dark in the room, but lights burning in the street outside made it possible to notice movement, focus on shapes. It helped that she had pale, almost porcelain skin, and that she was large with swollen, swinging breasts. And that she sat upright, slowly raising and lowering herself, making slapping sounds as the insides of her heavy thighs banged against his belly. He was only a dark shapeless thing that groaned. We all lay unmoving and concentrated.

Sex was often public in our one-bedroom Earls Court, London flat. It was unavoidable, and so became natural. At times there were six of us living in the small space, at other times, eighteen. We all came from far away, Australia, New Zealand, Africa. We came to London because the language and the culture made it a natural starting point for six months or a year of exotic European travel. We would work, party and tour: a sort of last hurrah before settling into a pleasant and predictable life back home. We were from new lands, we had few inhibitions, we were young.

Each morning I would walk past The Coleherne, an innocent, lifeless pub on the corner of our street, heading towards The Prince where I worked as a bartender, and each evening after closing I would return to my flat, passing again the pub on the corner of my street that was no longer lifeless or innocent. Men dressed in tight shiny black leather, and adorned with silver chains crowded the footpaths. Others were cruising slowly back and forth on Harley Davidson motorbikes, Ducats, Hondas, their small peaked leather caps set at rebellious angles. I was forced to weave a path through the eyeing, the caressing, the seducing. The Coleherne was a gay pub. I came from a small town that permitted no tolerance of homosexuality. I had never known a homosexual. I walked with care, defensively. Sometimes aggressively.

The Prince was a brewery-owned pub and the company had tried to create a warm, cosy atmosphere by using lots of pinks, floral-print wallpaper and a fake fire. It had a jukebox, pool table and two dartboards. The brewery was aiming for traditional English. The manager, a small Australian called Bruce, lived upstairs with his girlfriend and his dog, a long-haired German Shepherd that answered to the name of Digger.

Brian, our head barman, had allowed his chestnut coloured hair to grow long on one side in order to comb it across his balding top. He wore a thick, longish moustache, and had grown a little plump in his early middle age, but you hardly noticed as he moved quickly around the bar serving our heavy-drinking customers. Brian came from Yorkshire coal-mining country but his thick Northern accent had mixed with an assumed English upper class one, leaving you confused and charmed. His boyfriend was a lord. Brian was gay, but never in front of me, I wouldn't allow it.

We worked from eleven in the morning until eleven at night. Closed between three and five. Our clients were expatriate Scots, Irish, a few West Indians, colonials, and solid working or lower middle class English. They could be all things. Effusive or abusive, generous or rough. It was always a little unsettled around the pool table where the unsatisfactory rolling of the ivory balls often caused quarrels and sometimes more. When it was quiet we doubled as confessors, hearing intimate details of marital indiscretions, or boastings of sexual conquests. We would be told about difficult wives, or the state of someone's health, or the hardship brought about by poverty. We would discuss the merits of the local teams. We would make lasting friendships.

During the day older drinkers sat at our bar pushed out of their houses by loneliness. 'Have one yourself son!' In the evenings when the bar was always full, the crowd was more mixed, wilder. Women added their danger. 'A half please mate, three pints and a Johnny Walker short, give us a Guinness and three lagers. And have one yourself, and have one yourself!' You moved through the day alcohol-driven, racing faster and faster as the night crept on. And then I would walk back past The Coleherne, through the boys, turning often to glance over my shoulder, watching my back.

Digger, the long-haired German Shepherd, liked a beer. Bruce didn't approve. It was true that Digger could become aggressive when drunk, and the next day, hung-over, he was to be avoided. But it was never dangerous, you always knew when to stay clear; Digger would descend the staircase late in the morning leaning heavily against the wall to support himself, eyes bloodshot, dribbling a little.

Digger preferred Foster's. When he drank, unopened cans were placed on the bar by whoever Digger happened to be drinking with at the time. He would then stretch upwards, laying his front paws on the bar, balance himself, and then take the can in his mouth, drop back down, pierce it with his teeth, and slurp at the beer that fountained out.

One evening as I enjoyed a quick drink with Brian and Digger, I started to complain about The Coleherne, about 'the poofters'.

Peggy, a slight bubbly New Zealander with small breasts and cat-green eyes, overheard our conversation and squealed with delight. 'Take the homophobic bastard for a beer at The Coleherne, Brian. Yeah, take him for a beer,' she said, punching my shoulder, enjoying my discomfort. We had fucked the night before, and she had worn delicate paper panties that were a novelty fashion item in London in 1979. You could pull them apart with your teeth. In the morning I discovered that she had left deep scratch marks along my outside thighs and a small gash on my upper lip.

Two evenings later I stood at the long polished bar of a barren, almost gloomy pub, drinking pints with Brian. It was The Coleherne. All the drinkers were men, many wore thick falling moustaches and tight crotch-strangling leather pants. Others dressed in skin-hugging denim, and woodsman shirts. Handkerchiefs draped from their back pockets.

'What are the hankies for, Brian?' I asked innocently.

'Well,' he began, a little unsure if it was a good idea to tell me. 'I think if they are in the right pocket, they're active.'

'Active?' I asked.

'They do the fucking.'

'Oh!' I replied calmly.

'And the left side . . .' he continued.

'Passive,' I answered as if it were a test.

'Correct,' said Brian smiling, proud that I was not shocked. 'Now, red means just normal fucking, blue means fist fucking, yellow means watersport.'

'Watersport?'

'You know, pissing on each other.'

'Right,' I answered.

'I don't know whether it's right or left,' answered Brian, becoming flustered.

'No, I just meant I understood.'

74

'Fine,' he said, 'drink your beer.'

I did, we were both happy that the explanation had finished.

During the next few minutes we said little to each other. I sipped my beer and listened to the men talking around me, thinking all the while how suburban, ordinary the conversation was. I had expected depravity and filth, but got interiors and restaurants. There was flirting, touching of hands, subtle caressing, whispered secrets, but no groping or group ravishing.

Time passed and the beers started calming my heart that had been beating like a child banging at a drum. At times I would have to dextrously duck a cuddlesome arm, or elbow lightly a body that had moved too close, but my panic had disappeared.

'I'm leaving the pub, Brian, got a job on a building site. I can earn a lot more money.'

Brian raised his eyebrows to show his surprise before asking: 'When?'

'Next week,' I answered. Brian sucked on his cigarette, took a gulp of lager, pointed the cigarette at me and said, 'Still expect to see you as a customer, OK.'

When I first saw the huge man staring and snarling, I thought I was in for trouble. I moved closer to Brian who saw instantly where my discomfort came from. He turned to me, his upper lip curling into his moustache as he spoke, 'Watch out, they love small blonds.'

The man's beer disappeared into his ham fist as he grabbed it from the bar. He ran his other through his short-cropped hair as he lumbered towards us, wider and taller than any man he passed. His leather jacket opened to his navel, his chest which was matted with light curly hair was barrel shaped. As he neared our group broke apart allowing him space. He turned towards me, but looked past to a young man standing a little behind me and to my left, and in a voice that was higher and clearer than I expected greeted him knowingly.

'Peter, you're here.'

'You have a new beard,' replied Peter, not bothering to greet him back.

'Yes,' he smiled coyly, showing large uneven teeth . . . 'It's just long enough to lick, not quite long enough to bite yet.'

'So what did you think?' asked Brian as we left.

'Good blokes,' I replied.

'Not dangerous?' asked Brian smiling again.

'No mate, good blokes, but I'm still not going back for a drink without you.'

It was a Saturday night when the trouble began at The Prince, two days before I planned to leave and start working construction. It was freezing outside. In the afternoon it had rained and ice lay on the roads and footpaths, leaving them falling-down slippery. The pub was full of heavy-jacketed men, many still wearing their woollen caps. A warm dampness lifted from them as the pub heat sucked at their clothes. The jukebox blared, but you couldn't hear the words, you could barely make out the tune. There were fewer women than usual and they were mostly sitting around the tables towards the back where more air lurked. The pool table area was cluttered, you couldn't use the cues easily. That's where it began.

Robert, a small, gloss-black West Indian with strong shoulders and a short temper, lived for pool, made a living from it. And he wasn't given room to play. It was nobody's fault; there wasn't any room. Robert threw a terrific round right hand and busted a Scotsman's nose, who then fell back into his mate sending his full pint of beer sailing into the chest of Dennis, a Dubliner. When a chair was thrown from further down the bar, sailing, landing on the pool table, skidding off the balls, civilized instincts disappeared. Punches were thrown, shoving, pulling and scratching began. Men looked for enemies or something that could

76

pass for one. There were a lot of Glaswegians drinking that night. They waded in, clannish and content. We tried to drive, push them out onto the street, but there were few of us. Those that we got through the door stood swinging at each other, missing, falling, trying to rise, falling again, the ice whipping at their feet, and the alcohol spinning their bodies. Back inside a pimple-scarred shaven-headed English boy had broken a glass and was trying to slice open Brian's face.

'I was inches away from death,' Brian told later, 'barely holding his arm, the beer glass pushing towards me, when all of a sudden I feel a tap on my shoulder, another tap. I twist around and there's Jimmy.'

'Which Jimmy?' somebody screamed.

'Little Aussie Jimmy who only eats Guinness,' answered Brian annoyed, and continued. '"What?" I screamed. "What?" Jimmy stood behind me holding a telephone. The whole place is at war, and Jimmy's got a telephone.

'"Did anybody order a minicab, Brian?"

'I'm near death and he wants to know who ordered a minicab. A minicab,' he repeated disbelieving.

When the police arrived the fighting urge had cooled. Nobody was really hurt. It was not a gang fight and most people fight less bravely when they are alone. There were still scuffles but they quickly stopped. The glass-slicing boy who had been flattened by an arching right hand thrown by Bruce, our manager, scampered out with some of his mates like a rat down a sewer. Blood spewing from his badly cut lip. Some teeth missing. The Glaswegians also quickly disappeared. Many people were barred from The Prince.

The building site consisted of three, old, four-storey buildings that stood next to each other in Fulham. They were to be gutted and rebuilt. The boss and foreman were English. There were few tradesmen working at this stage of the project, it was mostly destruction, labourer's work. There were fourteen of us, twelve from Glasgow.

'I hate fuckin Aussies.'

The Glaswegian who had yelled out the insult sat on a dust-covered table, his back leant against a scarred, peeling wall. Next to him sat four other Glaswegians. All Prince drinkers. Sitting on the floor of the gutted room that was littered with hanging wire, ripped floorboards, new timber and cement bags, were more men eating thick white bread sandwiches, sipping scalding tea, and gazing at big-breasted women in dirt-soiled newspapers with hardly any text.

'Yea, and I hate fucking Scotsmen,' I answered back, realizing immediately that in a room full of Glaswegians that was about the silliest thing I could have said. I'm dead I thought. Where I came from, to be part of the mob meant you had to be tough, even if you were not, no way around it. What I said was not what I wanted to say, it was what I had been socially disciplined to say. But Willy saved me. His laugh filled the room, cut through the roughness, brought smiles to faces. 'Git sumpin tae eat,' he said, directing me with a nod of his head to a table where sausages lay in a blackened frying pan coated in thick old grease, and fried eggs, burnt around the edges, lay yolk running on unwashed plates beside piles of sliced white bread and squares of soft, food-stained butter. Huge pots of steaming tea, half-empty milk bottles, a rusting can full of white sugar and dirty tea mugs littered the rest of the table. A fry-up. I ate with relish. Willy sat down next to me, scratched at his thick red beard and pushed the long wiry hair that he sometimes wore in a ponytail towards me. 'They're jis pissed af ciz thir barred fae yir pub eftir the barney Setirday, they'll git owr it.'

I smiled and nodded, not believing him, and then asked, 'Do we get fed every day?'

'Ivrae day,' he grunted through a mouthful of sausage. 'Wit's yoor nem?'

'Macca,' I answered.

'Wee Macca,' he repeated aloud to no one, testing it on his tongue.

'Who pays for it?' I asked, when I saw he was satisfied with the sound it made.

'Management peys.'

'How?'

'Lid, that's wit they use tae insulate these aul' buildin's. The management sells it, if we dinnae steal it first.'

We were non-union labour working ten-hour days, a lot of high scaffold work, ripping out roofs, taking down crumbling chimneys, knocking through walls, digging out floors, sucking in thick nineteenth-century dust. Skips were filled and emptied, and filled again. A fry-up every morning and they paid cash.

The Glaswegians, all single men from the tough suburbs of a wild town, told me stories of axe woundings, machete slashings and hammer fights, as if they were part of a good Friday night out. Broken glasses were used as fists they guaranteed me. Every night they drank their fill and during our lunch break they drank their fill again.

Jacky, a thin, wasting, early-middle-aged man, brought a glass into an argument during one of these drinks in an Irish pub close to the building site. He was beaten badly and later hauled away by the police who didn't think it a normal thing to stick people with broken glass.

'Did ye help him?' asked Donald, the big rough, beer-bloated leader of the Scots, to the men who had been drinking with him.

'Nah, the wee bastard started the barney, an besides we dinnae wannae git barred, it's a gid pub tae huv a drink in.' Donald growled his agreement.

After lunch, work would become more dangerous. Timbers would be dropped, tools would slip from drunken hands, falls would be common. After one hard session, Willy brought a staircase down with a heavy sledgehammer, wild swings, and the power of five pints in an hour on an empty stomach. We all scampered like rabbits from the dogs. Another day, a three-metre steel support that was holding up a ceiling fell as the jack was knocked loose by a drunken stumble. It landed in a splash of dust, missing the men below by inches.

One Saturday morning overtime shift, cans of Scottish ale were smuggled in. We were laying a floor. We had just finished mixing and barrow pouring the too-wet cement. The beer took its effect. Two of the boys started arguing over a woman old enough to be their mother. Cans were thrown with venom, bouncing off walls, just missing heads, landing with plops in the fresh cement. Other Scots joined in as they always did. The English boss who stood at a safe distance behind a wall had to threaten to fire all of them before the argument stopped. The beer cans bobbed in the fresh-laid floor like floating rubbish in a water channel.

That same day I sat drinking tea and eating my sausage and egg sandwich on the floor with Davey, a slight man with neat short hair, a boyish face, and an unnatural calmness, even during the madness that happened around us. We had both laid our newsless papers to the side, and had not spoken for a few minutes, when I asked him how he managed to stay so untroubled and calm.

'Am yist tae it,' he explained. 'Uv seen sa much I doan't git excited. A grew up in Glasgow as well but a whant sumpin' mer than a drink in life, mer than jist bein' a hardman. A doano' whether a'll git it, wu'll see.' He blew into his tea that was already cold and continued. 'D'ye know wit Donald sid tae me the ither day, look at they drunks lyin' in the park, drinkin' and sleepin'. A think ad like a life lik 'at. A think he jis saw his ain future.'

I had met a girl. She had been down to London from Hull for the weekend. She was dark and university clever. Taller than myself. Olive skin, big breasts, posturing nipples. I was in love. In time I realized that it was not love, just an unconscious desire to improve the genes. But in the beginning it was love. I was paid well but I lived completely and that cost money, all of my money. We had planned a weekend together in two weeks' time. I was going to take her to see *Oliver!* at the London Palladium – that is if I could find the cash to pay for the ridiculously expensive tickets.

I saw it the day the police chased Donald up onto the roof. Dull dark silver, bent over itself, folded into a tight heavy bundle and lying behind a mound of broken bricks in a corner, almost hidden. Lead.

Donald came back to work the same day.

'Whit did ye dae, Donald?' asked one of the boys, smirking.

'I beet the shit oota a hoor who wiz touchin' up ma girlfriend.'

A chorus of whistles filled the workplace.

'Whin the fuck did you ever huv a girlfriend Donald?' came a voice from the back of the crowd. The whistles started again.

'A did, it wiz the wee lassie I met doon at the Fox,' he mumbled, dropping his head.

'At was no wee lassie, Donald, and you telt me you didnae even kiss her.'

'Well I planned tae, until a saw her last night wi 'at Saxon bastard. Anywae he wullnae be kissin her fur a while.'

'Why did you run, Donald?' I asked, 'there was no way out.'

He turned to me and smiled, the sheepishness gone. 'If you wur

Scoats you wid unnerstaun, we cannae be taken easy, even when wiv goat nae chance.'

That night, just after dark, I drove my van to the front of the house, kicked the unbolted door open, switched on my torch and went looking for the lead.

The scrap dealer gave me sixty pounds, a knowing look, and a strong handshake born from heaving and toting scrap metal bought under dubious circumstances. As I drove out of the yard I slowed at the gate and looked back. The dealer had taken off his cloth cap and was scratching his long wiry grey hair that sprang out over his ears but not on the top of his head. His two German Shepherd dogs sniffed at the lead suspiciously.

'Whir ra fuck is the lid? Who took 'e fuckin' lid?' Donald was shaking with rage, foaming at the mouth as he roamed through the building demanding an answer. Willy, who had been high on a scaffold working the roof when he heard the screaming, came down on the outside of the structure like a monkey chased out of a tree.

'Ra hoors huv stoalen oor fuckin' lid, Wullie, hoors, thuv stolen oor lid.'

'Sumdi stole the lid that we hid alriddy stolen,' repeated Willy to no one in particular, 'Ye cannae trust naebdy. Naebdy,' he said, shaking his head and bursting into laughter. 'Ye cannae trust naebdy.'

For the next four days I lived with fear. I had no idea that the lead had already been stolen. I thought it was management lead, fair game. I felt bad that I had cheated my workmates, but showing my tall Hull girl a good time meant more to me than doing the right thing by Willy and Donald. Besides, I reasoned, they would only drink it in and piss it against the wall. I was thinking about a future. Over the next few days they charged through the three buildings like wounded buffalo, accusing everybody directly. They threatened, cajoled, and in the end even pleaded, promising forgiveness, a drink, no hard feelings. But nobody trusted that. In their final frustration they accused the boss of stealing back his own lead.

I worked head down mouth shut, hoping my van had not been seen, and the scrap dealer was not the same one that Willy and Donald used. When my turn came to be accused, Willy stopped Donald. 'He's noh lik us, wee Macca's git a conshins, he widdnae steal oaf mates.'

My shame became larger than my fear. Shortly afterwards I left for another job, a renovation in Chelsea. A stockbroker's house, gold bath fittings, black Porsche out the front. The broker had married an American and she had wanted to mark an already beautiful house with her own scent. At times I would see my old workmates in The Prince. I would always be pulled into their noise and warmth. I would always leave swaying at closing.

'They're as mad as cut snakes,' I once said to Brian, 'dangerous to be with. I can't understand why I feel so comfortable with them.'

Brian smiled in his crooked sneering way, 'Your last name's McLennan, it's your heritage, they're your people.' He pulled a beer and pushed it towards me, 'Ye poor silly bastard. Besides, would you be rather drinking with the boys down at The Coleherne?'

ROWING TO ALASKA

The rain came down so thickly that the water-pregnant clouds that carried it were camouflaged and hidden high above. The bare, breast-shaped hills that were pockmarked with tree stumps became muddy and slick. Streams appeared, gullies formed. A cold and miserable greyness shrouded the landscape, suffocating optimism.

Doug appeared two metres to my left, his thick glasses and wet straggly moustache his only recognizable features above his covering of yellow wet-weather gear. His movements were slow and precise as he climbed upwards. Every second moment his right hand, which held a long wooden-handled mattock, would slash down through the wetness and gouge a hole into the soft ground, while his left hand plucked a spruce plant out of a soaking mud-weighted bag that was strapped to his back. In one movement the plant was rooted into the ground and held in place by dirt that Doug would heel in. He would then take three steps forward and repeat the planting. And I would attempt to do the same.

The beer tasted sour and weak, but I drank it anyway. They only sold beer in the tavern. Doug, who drank cautiously, spoke in the same way, 'You warmed up yet? It's no way to start your first day

84

of tree planting with slick boots and no wet-weather gear, not up in this country where it rains more than it shines. You looked like a walking drowned man. I ain't never seen anybody shaking so much.'

I had found the job the day before through a man who had picked me up hitch-hiking outside Portland, Oregon. We had driven together to Olympia in Washington State, and I was now working for his brother-in-law, John Mulverhill at Forest Renewal Management, for four dollars and seventy-five cents an hour.

Doug stood by the bar staring at the pool table, wondering about his last shot, not understanding how he had missed. 'Not such bad country up here?' he finally asked after his long contemplation of the balls that he had just played. He seemed to be speaking to somebody else. I looked around before I answered. The jukebox was flashing light and filling the bar with a Dr Hook tune, the cigarette smoke united and became a blue-grey mist held by the low ceiling. Drinkers who looked like bikers, but who I knew to be woodsmen either killing trees or planting them, crowded the bar and occupied the pool tables, swilling their Budweisers from the bottle, dry and happy. Young women wearing tight jeans flittered in and out with trays of beer, occasionally rubbing against you, giving you hope.

'She'll do, mate,' I finally answered, 'she'll do.'

I worked two months planting spruce saplings in country that climbed so high it pushed through the low-slung clouds. Cold rain was thrown at you constantly like pebbles at a stray dog. We lived in mud. But on occasions the sun would shine and the warmth would lift the wetness from you in a vapour, light would be refracted from the dampness and the world would begin to sparkle, deer would walk near as if they were just part of the work crew. Men would laugh.

Doug became a good mate during this time. He taught me the planting technique, hole, plant, bury, three paces, repeat, and he showed me how to hide trees under fallen logs to keep production up and convince the foreman – who screamed a little too much instead of watching more closely – that we were damn quick workers. At midday break when the weather allowed we would light a fire and heat water for coffee. Tree bags which weighed thirty pounds were downed for an hour and the crew would fall around the fire to warm. The foreman drank his coffee alone. He wasn't welcome.

It was during one of these breaks that Tommy, a grey-bearded, middle-aged drifter who always spoke with eyes pointing downward, slurped his too hot coffee and told us a story about the Alaska gold rush. 'Men became mad, crazy for gold,' he began, 'they came from every state in the Union, wharf labourers and clerks from New York, Boston, farmers from the Midwest, or south of the Mason–Dixon Line, cowboys from Montana, Wyoming, Texas, poor men, adventurers, thieves and profiteers. They came from all walks of life, all heading to Alaska. Some crossed the continent from east to west, others caught ships that sailed down the East Coast, and passed through the Panama Canal before heading north to San Francisco or Seattle. Everybody was heading for Skagway, from where they could cross over the mountains to the goldfields and fortune.

'For men with money it wasn't a problem getting to Skagway, but for others it was a desperate time. Food supplies, tents, blankets, mining equipment, bars, shovels, gold-pans and mercury had to be bought, and the prices had been pushed sky-high by the gold seekers crowding the stores. Tickets going north were expensive, boats had to be shared with cattle, horses and freight. A lot of men were forced to try it on their own. Small boats were built or bought. Sailboats, canoes, rowing dories. Some were worm-riddled, rotting, unseaworthy, and the men that set out never had a chance of arriving. Others were good boats handled by men who understood tides, weather and charts. These carried their passengers all the way to Skagway. The sailboats could make it in a month, but the rowers took two and a half months to pull the one thousand two hundred miles. Sometimes a line would be thrown from a passing ship and they could hook a ride, but that wasn't often.'

I can't remember whose idea it was, whose heart first beat faster, who made the other excited, but at some point during our time working as tree planters in the forests of Washington State, Doug and I decided to row a boat to Alaska.

The planting had finished and now we sat slowly sipping tin-tasting Budweiser beer in the small prefabricated home of Jack Waterman, our lead planter and hero since he had told the foreman 'to go fuck himself' the day before. Jack's Nez Percé Indian wife Charleyne stood frying pancakes for everybody on their two-burner gas stove.

'What's this I hear about you rowing a boat to Alaska?' asked Sid Beachworth, the father figure in our crew, as he carefully measured and poured our first glass of after-dinner Jack Daniel's. 'It don't make sense.'

'What don't make sense?' answered Doug defensively.

'Well,' continued Sid, who had a fierce drinking face gouged with lines that could only have come from laughing, 'it will take you a long time, time that you could be using to work, to start a career, getting on with life, not wasting it. Besides it's been done before.'

'That was a long time ago and not by an Australian,' I said.

'Wish the hell I was going,' yelled Jack from the other side of the room where he had been changing a country song for another country song. 'As far as I see it, it don't have to make sense.'

Sid smiled, deepening his face ravines. 'I guess I'm just getting old,' he offered in his good-natured way, raised his glass of Jack Daniel's and wished us the best. We all drank.

Seattle was built on a neck of land between the Puget Sound and Lake Washington. To the west climb the Olympic Mountains, protecting Seattle from heavy winter rains that race in from the sea. To the east, the Cascade Mountains shield it from the great heat and cold that breeds in mid-continental America. It is completely married to the surrounding wilderness. A pearl in a blue-and-green shell. It was born as a mill town, but its protected harbour and geographical location allowed it to blossom as a centre of trade to the Orient and Alaska. The harbour is constantly full of large ships, emptying and loading, or just swinging around on their anchor lines waiting their turn at the dock like milling cattle needing to be milked. The clean, tall, modern city stands gazing down. Seattle was the place we chose to start our trip.

We found a small basement apartment at an address downtown, close to the water. The bad part of Seattle, or so we were told. The apartment block was managed by an ex-army colonel, who wore a goatee beard and played saxophone in a band. He walked with a crippling limp, the result of being blown up in Vietnam. He had no regrets he told us, for him the threat of a communist sweep through South-East Asia was real and worth defending against. He gave us the apartment without a bond, he thought Doug looked trustworthy.

There are many considerations when you decide to row a boat to Alaska, and we had considered very few of them, but when you consider too much it often becomes too much. Off we went. Doug, who was from Colorado with a bachelor's degree in biology, found a job changing truck tyres, and I, working under the imposition of having no green card, became head dishwasher at Steve's All-

Night Broiler, a restaurant owned by three Greek brothers: Stefanos, Costas and Georgios.

We found a boat builder called Mr Polak who had large thick hands and a short-sightedness that left him stumbling and tripping like a new-born foal. He worked from a town named Carnation, a Dutch immigrant community nestled in dairy-farming country thirty miles to the east of Seattle. We settled on a price of one hundred dollars a foot. Mr Polak would build us a Grand Banks dory, twenty-two feet long, made from Douglas fir and powered by ash oars. It would be beautiful and unsinkable, he assured us, and if we wanted to row it to Australia, he would guarantee it, but would not accompany us.

By day I would be filling a steaming stainless-steel machine with egg-splattered, meat-soiled, mayonnaise-glued dishes, and at night we would be looking for the right food to take on the voyage, attending sales talks on newly produced dry goods, scouring the papers for second-hand camping equipment and safety gear. We bought books on currents, tides, charts of the passage, books about mammals, birds, we read about bear, whale, deer. We learned to use a compass, a camera, and we played. Or rather, I played. Doug was a one-woman man, solid and old-fashioned, somebody who respected tradition, correctness, he stayed loyal to his girlfriend who was still studying at his old university, three thousand miles away in Denver, Colorado.

Steve's Broiler ran all day and night. The three Greek brothers would each manage one of the eight-hour shifts, always there, watching. With thickly accented English and a powerful first-generation work ethic, they were calmly, completely in control. Each shift they employed one dishwasher, two short-order cooks, and three waitresses. At the back of the restaurant they had opened a cocktail bar that was gloomy and comfortable.

At Steve's, the coffee refills were free and the long counter always full. The cooks dressed in white, pulled orders, fried eggs – over easy or sunny side up – crisped bacon, browned hash browns, toasted bread, sizzled sausage – three orders at a time. The waitresses, dressed in their short pink-checked skirts, moved around and between the fake red-leather covered booths, serving food at a pace that mesmerized their clients, and I rinsed and rinsed, before stacking my machine with dishes, cups, pots and pans, and stared through the opening by the sink at madness.

At times, as in all public business, there was trouble. The bacon was not crisp, the order would be wrong, the egg not exactly right, the coffee cold. Sometimes people just want trouble. In the worst cases the police were called, at other times the cooks and dishwasher were sufficient, but mostly the waitresses took care of the problem. They would pet the troublemakers like doting mothers, cajole them like a schoolmistress, or scream and threaten them like a shrewish wife. One evening Cheryl, a half Sioux Indian with wavy, thick black hair, deep dark eyes and the bewitching beauty of a tropical flower in a weed garden, was serving coffee to a man who had left his penis hanging out of his pants as an invitation. Without a word she poured the hot coffee directly onto his balls. That night only an ambulance was needed.

We had decided on dried food for our trip. It was light, affordable, and the salesman assured us it was nutritious. Just add water. Bulk was a problem, space a premium, we needed so much that it was impossible to carry it all. We solved this by arranging to have three boxes of food flown to a town at the northern end of Vancouver Island in Canada, and another load to Ketchikan, Alaska. We bought a second-hand tent, new sleeping bags, pots and pans, cups, a small gas-burner, gas bottles – we planned to cook as much as possible on open fires – one survival suit, they were just too expensive, and a radio receiver, no sender, the same reason. Rain gear, ropes, jackets, knives, fishing tackle, chain and anchor. Doug taught me to cook chilli con carne with cornbread, heavily spiced.

Every few weeks we would check the progress of our boat and we would always find Mr Polak stumbling around, hammering this, screwing that, heating struts to bend, or shaving timber, the cold air in his unheated shed heavily polluted with wood dust. He would rush over to us, excited and proud of how the boat was coming along, his large hands almost breaking ours with his welcome.

In the beginning the *Renee Blue*, as we had named her, looked inelegant and flimsy, a large animal that had been picked clean of flesh. But over time Mr Polak built in a strength and pride. You could see her taking shape, like a hollow-chested boy turning into a man; the double ends that were characteristic of a Grand Banks dory rising high and fine, the ribs filling in.

On one of these inspections we bought a gun. We had thought a lot about it, we had talked to many people. 'Would we need a gun?'

'Where there is bear you need a gun, and if you don't fire it, it's still damn nice to know that you could have if needed,' so explained Mr Polak, who liked guns.

The gun shop was next door to the boat building shop. For two hundred and fifty US dollars, no identification necessary, we bought an Ithaca twelve-gauge pump action shotgun that fired eight cartridges. We were advised to alternate the cartridges with slugs for bears and shot for birds. We did.

We were constantly unpacking and repacking our equipment, making the size and order right. We had bought waterproof bags that could be packed away in storage space that Mr Polak was building at the front and back of our boat. We were getting nearer.

The preparations were expensive, much more than we thought. I took another job as a cleaner in the Bell Telephone Building, inventing a social security number and a history to explain my

Australian accent. I worked almost three months under this lie and each week I received my pay cheque and pay slip with my name correctly spelled and my fake security number printed neatly above, all tax deductions listed. Near the end of my employment I considered applying for a tax rebate, but was advised by Doug that that might be pushing my luck.

By the middle of June the *Renee Blue* was finished. Mr Polak had sanded and joined his last timber, his paintbrushes were stiff, hard, used and useless, his tools lay scattered on benches or half hidden amongst discarded wood and half empty paint and varnish tins, unwanted and ignored. The *Renee Blue* rested on low scaffolding that in turn rested on a bed of sawdust. She had been painted bright red and her name had been drawn on each side of the bow in white. The ash oars that had been coated three times with varnish leaned against the far wall waiting to go to work.

The *Renee Blue* was wrapped in ropes that were run through pulleys and then raised until her bed of scaffolding could be knocked out of the way and a trailer reversed under.

Once sitting comfortably, she was pulled through the streets to the cheers of beer-swilling villagers who had come to watch, and then down to the river which passed beside the town to begin her journey, first to Seattle harbour and then to Alaska a thousand miles away.

We drove to our apartment and back to the now floating *Renee Blue* in Mr Polak's Dodge pick-up, loading and unloading. By midday she was packed, our anchor was tied on, our goodbyes were said, and we solemnly accepted the good lucks offered to us. Down we sat, side by side, and away we pulled, and pulled. Mr Polak and a few village people watched, smiling and waving. But something was wrong; the *Renee* would not row straight. I thought it must be Doug pulling too hard and he thought it must be me. As we sat next to each other, each in control of one oar, each pulling harder and harder, snarling, Mr Polak started screaming from the shore, 'It's the ballast, we forgot the ballast.'

The *Renee Blue* was unloaded, the floor hatch pulled up and gravel from the shore shovelled in.

'More weight on top of the one thousand two hundred pounds we already have to pull,' groaned Doug, wiping raindrops from his face with the back of his hand, smiling crookedly. It was deep into the afternoon when we finally rowed out of sight of our gang. It was dark and still wet when we stumbled ashore exhausted, pushed our boat out to anchor and set up camp that first night. We pegged our tent out on the beach, laid out the sleeping bags, primed and lit the gas stove, cooked our first dry food meal, a chewy beef stroganoff, sipped our coffee, and I smoked. We felt content and confident heading towards Alaska. That night we were washed out of our tent by the incoming tide. But we were lucky, the weather was gentle, and we only lost a little food.

The next days brought blisters and beards. My hands had become so scarred that I could barely hold the oars, and my arse little better as it skidded across the seat in time with the rowing motion. I remembered a home remedy that I had used to harden my hands when I was boxing a few years before, so every morning before taking up the oars I would piss on them. Doug was in no better shape, but it was hard to tell because he complained a lot less.

We moved slowly, pulling in time with each other across the gentle rain-flattened water towards the north. The Juan de Fuca Strait, a tongue of water separating Vancouver Island and a slip of mainland, threw the Pacific at us in swells one after another. The *Renee Blue* rode up and down, balanced and sturdy.

Further we went, snaking through the San Juan and then the

Gulf Islands, heading for Nanaimo on Vancouver Island. Tall evergreen-smothered inlets, with rock-strewn sandy beaches, became our home, splashes of painted wildflowers surrounded our tent. The *Renee Blue* waited patiently, riding on water as smooth as oiled steel.

Sometimes we would get lost in the greyness because the rain would not stop and the islands that were as thick as roosting gulls would never match the islands on our charts, then we would ask a cruiser because we saw many small boats on this part of our trip.

'Where are you going?' they would always ask.

'Alaska,' we would shout back. A smile always came to their faces. Doug always called it a smirk.

We passed on good terms through the Canadian Immigration and Customs, which was just a small office built on a low cliff overlooking a rock-spotted cove on an unspectacular island. Our inspector, a small round man in a sharply ironed uniform, had visited Australia in 1954 with the Canadian navy. It had been during the visit of our newly crowned Queen Elizabeth II, and he was a fierce believer in the Commonwealth and a great admirer of Elizabeth. I convinced him that I was too, and that we were brothers under our queen. Our boat was never checked and the shotgun we had decided not to declare was never found.

We reached Nanaimo after eight days, but rowed uncaringly past. From the sea it looked large and unloved, and we had grown used to astounding beauty. We would wait until the town of Campbell River for the pleasures of civilization.

Clouds smothered the sun, but it had stopped raining. Our blisters had broken and hardened and my beard had thickened. Doug continued to shave. We were pulling next to each other as if born with an oar in our hands. The *Renee Blue* cut a reasonably straight line through the sea as she headed north. At the end of each day we would fight the waves that came with the change of weather, struggling to keep the boat from being bashed on the beach by surf as we unloaded our gear. Afterwards, Doug or I would strip, and swim the boat out beyond the surf line to anchor her. Before making camp we would light a fire from the driftwood that lay everywhere and dry ourselves. We began to eat more and more.

We had planned on harvesting shellfish but they had become polluted. A red tide, a bad bacteria, had invaded the coast. We trailed a line behind us as we rowed hoping to entice salmon but our pace was too slow and we caught very few fish. In the evening we were too tired to fish, or too lazy. When we reached Campbell River we were low on food.

It was at Campbell River that we had arranged to have some of our dry food flown in. We picked up three boxes from the office of Northern Freighters, a small transport company that delivered to Canada and Alaska. Later, when the food was packed away and our hunger unbearable, we found a small cafe decorated with two mounted salmon and a stuffed, medium-sized black bear, and sat at tables covered with plastic green-checked tablecloths. When the waitress, a plump middle-aged woman with dyed-red hair and deep cleavage, brought our order of bacon, eggs over easy, hash browns, pancakes and syrup, she hovered around us like a worried mother, filling our coffee cups and listening to our stories of seas and storms. When we ordered the same again she had the cook pile on the food so high that the pancakes slipped from the plate, dribbling syrup onto the check tablecloths. That evening we found a bar, its dark lighting forcing us to squint as we entered. Old, stale beer smells assaulted us. Drinking noise echoed, smothering familiar conversation. Heat from the wool-clad drinkers warmed the air. We drank Molsen beer with the locals and wobbled out at closing time.

'Watch out for Seymour Narrows,' was their warning as we wished them goodnight.

'Good sense and judgement are necessary qualities to use when making a trip through the Northwest Passage to Alaska,' or so we had read. But at times undependable emotion makes the important decisions. There are tools provided for people boating to Alaska that help you make qualified decisions: charts and compass for navigation, information about tide changes, directions of currents. These things are most important because there are places along the way where twenty-foot tides rush through narrow passages, moulding violent whirlpools that can suck a small boat under. If you move through these dangerous waters at slack tide, when it is not coming in or going out, then there is no danger.

We woke hung-over and restless. The Canadian beers which tasted of chemicals had soiled our stomachs and boxed with our heads, leaving us uncoordinated. Doug checked the tide tables. It was another three hours to slack. Seymour Narrows, a mile-long tunnel of water that at the wrong time sped between steep cliffs at fifteen knots, waited for us three miles further up. To leave now meant we would be travelling at the most dangerous time.

'We can eat and take it easy,' I suggested.

'I'm damn sure hung-over,' Doug answered after a long pause, 'Let's get out of this town.'

We loosed our lines and started moving quickly towards the narrows, at five knots. There was no need to row, we used our oars only to guide the boat. It was still early morning and it had begun to rain heavily. We found the entrance amongst the confusion of islands and reefs. Trees growing on the cliffs on both sides were entwined with clouds that hung like grey lace shawls, shutting out light. The black-and-white water in the narrows was jumping, twisting, bumping like a crowd in a busy city, limiting our view.

We could see that the sides were calmer, the water had more room, it flowed quickly, but composed. We pointed the *Renee Blue* and headed into the passage, moving faster and faster.

The freighter appeared through the downpour as a large animal sometimes appears in the night before your headlights. It had also chosen the side of the narrows. It towered over us, pushing towards us against the rushing current, forcing a wall of water to stand out on both sides of the bow. We were jostled towards the centre of the passage, towards the whirlpools. The wall of water that stood ten feet high crashed down on us as we hung on. The *Renee* filled, an oar washed overboard, we had lost the last piece of control we had. The white circling pools that were as large as a room sucked at the boat and spun her round and round, at the same time thrusting us through the passage. All we could do was sit on the bottom of the boat and cling. The *Renee Blue* was thrown from one whirlpool to the next, finally slowing and turning like the last pirouette of a dying ballerina. Our oar had made the trip with us and I was able to scoop it up as we were spat out at the end of the ride.

We rowed heavily to a dock that belonged to a small fishing community built at the end of the narrows. The *Renee Blue* was three quarters full of seawater but the watertight compartments that Mr Polak had built in her structure had saved us. Gear floated around in the bottom of the boat. As I searched for a smoke that hadn't been soaked, I asked Doug why he thought we should have tried the passage when it was running at its quickest.

'Well, I don't understand myself,' he thoughtfully replied, 'I just needed to get going, probably just drank too much the night before. Besides,' he pointed out as he pushed the plunger down on the plastic pump and watched thick gushes of water dive back into the bay, 'you could have said no.'

'But I drank more than you did, Doug,' I answered, shivering.

A sharply angled white boat with two powerful outboard motors raced towards the passage, saw us bailing and swung violently towards us. It spun to a stop, its wake banging the *Renee Blue* against the dock. It flew a large Canadian flag and *coastguard* was clearly written in red on one side.

'Did you see anybody sink in the narrows?' he screamed down at us, from his position high up behind the wheel of his boat. 'We got a message from a freighter that they had sunk somebody.'

'No, mate,' I replied, continuing my bailing.

'We didn't see a thing, sir,' added Doug, who was always more formal.

'Where did you two just come from then?' he asked suspiciously.

'Seymour Narrows,' answered Doug, not looking up from his pumping.

Canadians are famously more paternal than Americans. Like their colonial parents, the British, officials take a much greater interest in the personal safety of their people. They make laws to discourage risk-taking. The police were infamous during the Alaskan and Yukon gold rush for stopping miners from setting out to the goldfields during the winter months, or from travelling the rivers before the spring floods caused by melting ice had slowed. Our coastguard man felt the same responsibility and lectured us about the stupidity of what we had just done and the dangers that lay ahead. Better quit, was his advice.

'Is there a law to stop us from going on?' I asked, stopping my work for a moment to relight my cigar that was still damp.

'No,' he replied quickly, 'but my advice is to quit.'

'Then we'll go on,' answered Doug, losing his formality, 'We're sorry you were called out, but we didn't make the call.'

The bay was full of logs jammed together. In the woods behind the shoreline, nestled among the towering timbers, were wooden houses.

They were spread out in no formal order but their design was specific, they were built to shelter large numbers of people. A tiny man stood on the jetty waiting for us. As we neared, he reached out and took the rope that I had thrown out to him. His name was Peter Connelly. He was four feet nine inches tall and moved with a low-to-the-ground quickness that dazzled you. Peter was a logger. He was guarding the camp while the rest of his crew took a break, and his round cheery face showed just how happy he was to have company.

'I'm forty-four,' he told us as he served up our second helping of steak and mashed potato. 'I've been working in logging camps since I was thirteen, so that would be,' he thought a moment, 'thirty-one years.

'I've done about everything in a logging camp, that is except climb the trees, couldn't ever take the heights. But now this belly of mine starts to get in the way so I do a lot of odd jobs around the camp, the kitchen, keeping the place looking a bit civilized, that sort of thing.'

'What do you do when the camp is empty?' asked Doug, still digging into his mashed potato like a starving man.

'I read,' replied Peter. 'Only learned when I was thirty, but now look at this.' He showed us a thick book, a Louis L'Amour cowboy story, 'I love 'em.'

That evening, sitting at the long dinner table before an open fire that dominated the canteen, we drank coffee and sipped from the whisky bottle that Peter had brought out. Peter played sad Canadian ballads on his harmonica, leaving us feeling warm and safe, and strangely reminding us of faraway places.

'What about women, Peter?' I asked as his music died away. Doug looked at me and moved his head ever so slightly left and right. Peter scratched at his unshaven neck. 'I had a girl once,' he told us, 'but she drank, so did I in those days, a lot. We would always end up fighting, throwing things. Once she called me a worthless little imp and pulled a gun on me. I had to hit her, I never went back. Now I just pay for my women. It's a little sadder but a lot safer. Nanaimo has a lot of women who take care of men like me.'

The next morning after a breakfast we rowed quietly away. Peter sat on the jetty, short legs teasing the water, waving us seaward.

We moved slowly along a stretch of water called the Johnstone Strait, fighting the wind that blew at the *Renee Blue*'s nose. We were in choppy sea, not rough, but it hid our view of the dolphins until they were almost on top of us. Even when they were surrounding the boat their black bodies disappeared into the darkness of the water, but every now and then as they butterflied past, you could glimpse their white undersides, you could see two black streaks running from their eye down into the whiteness below. There were over thirty of them.

'Striped dolphin,' said Doug, without being asked. I acknowledged his answer with a nod and a grin and we rowed on.

The small inlet looked full wine-glass calm as we pulled out of the strait after noticing huts built just back from the water.

'Must be another logging camp,' muttered Doug.

'Good food,' I answered. 'Let's have a look, test the hospitality.'

There were no logs jamming the water; Doug thought they had probably hauled them away. The men who stood around the shore watching us row in were work-muscled and rough-looking. It was a warm day out of the wind and most wore T-shirts and almost all were heavily tattooed. There was no jetty and no other boats. As we moved closer we called out a greeting but got no reply. As I stepped ashore the men moved back to let a man through who had just arrived. He was heavy-set, but seemed less threatening than the others. His full black beard almost hid the large smile he gave us in welcome. 'My name's Jacob,' he offered, and then, 'Where's your boat?'

'This is our boat,' replied Doug, pointing at the *Renee Blue*. He turned to look at the other men, and then back to us as if somebody was playing a trick on him. 'Where are you coming from?' he finally asked.

'Seattle,' I replied, grinning at their confusion.

'You rowed two hundred miles?' asked one of the tattooed men.

'Yeah,' I answered, 'took us two weeks. Got a cigarette, mate?'

The tattooed man threw me his tobacco pouch. Jacob and the others wandered closer to look at the *Renee Blue*. Finally Jacob turned back to us, 'You must be hungry, let's eat.'

As we walked up the hill towards the metal huts that had been built on a large dust-layered clearing, Jacob, towering over us, spoke, 'Did you know this is a corrective work-camp?'

'A jail,' translated Doug, more for himself than me.

'But don't worry,' Jacob continued, 'the worst we got here is an armed bank robber, and he got caught easy.'

Over a lunch of cold meats, salads and potatoes, Jacob explained to us that it was a low-security corrective centre. 'These men are here to be rehabilitated, they thin young trees, chainsaw work, and they get paid nine dollars a day.'

'What about escapes?' I asked, perplexed at the lack of confinement.

'Well, there's a dirt road out of here, but we are in the middle of nowhere. I've got the only vehicle, and besides Vancouver Island is just that, an island. We would always get them and they know it.'

'Are you the only guard?'

'I'm not really a guard,' he explained, 'I'm more a work foreman. They police themselves, and yes, there are two of us. Norman, he's in Nanaimo buying supplies.'

As we sat eating, a tall thin man with long, stringy brown hair and daggers and hearts tattooed on both forearms came to our table. 'A few of us have been talking,' he began without introducing himself, 'we're gunna build you a mast, make a sail.'

We spent three days in the work camp. We slept in our own tent but ate all our meals with the inmates. The cook, who was a little older than the rest and seemed more at home with his role as prisoner, served us crab, steak and even lobster. His breakfasts were as good as those in Steve's Broiler, and like all good cooks he would flutter around the tables demanding approval of his meals. He was the bank robber. Daggers and hearts, we found out, was there for robbery and assault. Newfy, his mate, a shaven-headed Newfoundlander, who always put me in mind of a grinning bear, had been in and out of jail since he was a kid. He was sewing the sail. There were three others in the group; along with the cook they were at the top of the camp hierarchy. They sat at the head table, received food first, worked on the easiest slopes. Once, before I understood, I sat without thinking in a seat used by a group member. I was quickly warned out. I also had to play by their rules.

It was the rules that kept the peace, the rules were made by the strongest but that was no different than other places I had been. I saw no aggression, but was told by Jacob that fights occurred. 'As long as they don't kill each other, we stay out of it.'

Our trip became very important to a lot of the prisoners. We would go over the places we had been, the weather conditions, sea conditions, what lay ahead. Our charts would be pored over in detail, and dangers pointed out. When we mentioned a town we planned on visiting, we were told where to drink and where not to, the quality of the girls and the trouble involved in catching them. It seemed important to them that we not run into problems, that we reach Juneau, that we succeed. We were never given an address to stay.

'We only know people as bad as ourselves,' Newfy once told me.

The mast had been carved with care. Newfy had used old, colourless canvas for the sail, he had gouged eyeholes and attached the sail to the mast with ropes and a crossbeam. More ropes had been attached for the positioning of the sail. We packed it securely down the side of the boat before saying our goodbyes. Daggers gave me a parcel – 'Tobacco and food for the trip,' he grunted. Cook stood a little up the hill, arms folded, smiling. We received a warning from Newfy not to use the sail in big winds. A lot of the boys had come to watch us leave. They squatted down, waiting until we had rowed out into the chop of the channel and out of sight.

After the prison we crossed over to the mainland, dancing through the small islands that still crowded the Johnstone Strait, and then hugged the coast to start our pull up the Queen Charlotte Sound.

We fashioned a new system for anchoring out. The anchor and its rope and chain were left sitting on the bow, another rope was fastened to the anchor. After unloading we would push the boat out past the tideline. The anchor was then tugged from the *Renee Blue* with the second rope. At times we misjudged the distance. One morning we found the *Renee Blue* standing vertical against a large boulder as if leaning patiently on the bar waiting to be served. Twice we woke just in time to see the tide trickle past her sides, leaving her rock-stranded for six hours.

Thick fog; a grey wet wall sat around us. Water flooded our faces, Doug licked his moustache continually. I squeezed droplets out of my thick beard until they formed a stream and then fell, cascading to my chest. We had been rowing blind for two hours when we finally agreed that we should lay out the compass to check direction. We had been rowing to Japan.

Along the Queen Charlotte Sound we camped much of the time in inlets, coves when we could reach them. Calm peaceful places that usually had good driftwood for fire, and sometimes a stream to fill our water tanks. At other times we were left to the open beach, our boat bobbing upon waves that had already travelled thousands of miles. During those nights we slept in the *Renee Blue*, careful that she wasn't washed away.

Mornings were often damp and hazy but it cleared in the afternoons when the west wind cleansed the sky and made rowing rough, thumping water into us until our shoulders burned and our backs cramped. When you looked to the shore the trees came down to the sea edge. Two powerful natures resigned to stalemate.

Once we saw an Alaskan ferry racing by, and once a stumpy, thick-shouldered tugboat pulling loaded barges, parting the water as if it were a sharpened knife slicing paper. But the small pleasure boats were gone. Sea otters with heads like old men stretched out of the waves to look at us. Eagles hunted the shores.

We bounced around Cape Caution, shoved and pushed in many directions by a confused sea that became more so when the strong winds and ebbing tide fought, past Allison Harbour and into the Inside Passage, a great piece of open sea behind us. Our hands had callused and our bodies were lean and fit. We had been travelling for a month.

It was like standing in a gallery admiring a painting for a very long time and then moving to the next. You could clearly see it was the same artist, the familiarity was unmistakable, but it was as if one had been painted with the left hand, and the other with the right.

The forest that crowded the shoreline and the rocky headlands, that appeared black and secretive, started climbing. Mountains loomed, some fringed in green, others still capped in frozen white.

My hands had started to cramp during the cool of the night. Each morning I would have to pry my fingers open one by one. Doug had started mixing egg powder, flour and water together to make dumplings to add to our packaged food. Each evening after our gear was unloaded, one of us would swim the *Renee Blue* out in freezing water to anchor. We had given up on the two-rope system.

We rowed on past the Haida Indian village of Namu, past the fishing boats that bobbed at the docks waiting to unload at the cannery that employed the town – which had been built high on wooden legs to protect it from the tides. It was low tide when we passed and all the buildings stood uncomfortably in rubbish-polluted mud. An Indian boy wearing a Yankees baseball cap came down to the dock and waved us past.

The channel was narrow and we were protected from westerlies and southerlies, but the currents forced us to row in a rhythm, to follow the moon. Doug talked with yearning about growing old and having a good rocking chair and fine memories. My tobacco was almost finished.

We reached Bella Bella, another Haida community, as daylight faded to late afternoon dimness. But there was no store. As we walked along the dock towards the neatly-spaced wooden houses that perched on higher ground amongst the timber, a man called out from his seat on his front steps that my blond hair would make a good scalp. He touched a knife that he wore on his belt as he spoke, others became caught up in the joke, their laughter ate away the quiet. We walked slowly around the town, uncomfortable about being white amongst a people who had complaints about their treatment in history. Many men were drinking, some were drunk, others unconscious.

'A plane landed with alcohol.'

I looked behind me to see a heavy, serious woman wearing a spotless white T-shirt and pressed blue jeans.

'Normally this is a dry town,' she continued. 'Drinking can be a problem here. If you want supplies, row across the bay. It's a white-run store,' she added, dropping her head in embarrassment. After buying cigarettes we rowed quietly out of Bella Bella. We preferred to camp in peace.

The bear was only fifteen feet away, her cinnamon colour blending into the shadows thrown by the tall firs, blurring her, disguising her. We were gliding by on a glass backwater, she could hear us, she followed a few metres, stood and glared at the water. She was not big – black bears seldom are – but she was powerful and curious. We pulled a little harder, putting distance between us, watched her drop back down to her four feet and lose interest.

The southerly was steady and solid, the waves rolling but even. Today the Milbanke Sound was kind. Doug spat a glob of chewing tobacco from the side of his mouth, staining his chin, missing the water. It fell solidly, landing at his feet on the bottom of the boat.

'Let's try that sail,' he said, giving me a wink and a brown, mushy grin. We set the mast, laid up the crossbeam and quickly unfurled it. We tied off on one side and hand-held the other sail rope to position it to the wind. We lashed our two oars together as a rudder and began to fly. They had made us a square sail which could be tilted to catch a following wind, but one which you could not tack with. We used it only once, the wind was never just right again.

Past the village of Klemtu, past Butedale, past cascading waterfalls dropping through the trees, foaming, spitting out fine white spray, splashing rainbows in the air. Between mountains that loomed down on us on both sides like powerful, old, white-haired men, amused at our travels. Past valleys that had been ripped out of the mountain by glacial meanderings, and out into the sea before the town of Prince Rupert.

There the roar of fast cars, souped-up engines and shortened exhausts drifted down to the docks where we were busy tying off the *Renee Blue* and packing away loose gear. This was the first town with a road leading somewhere since Campbell River on Vancouver Island and the last one we would come across as we headed north.

When we first pulled in it had been drizzling, now the rain began to have more weight and purpose.

'Where are you guys planning to sleep tonight?' came a deep, friendly voice from above. I looked up at a man with thick dark hair.

'In the boat,' I answered.

'It's real wet, bro. Come and stay up at the house, it's not much but it's dry.' That night in a weatherboard house at the back of town, we drank with Robert and his mates. Some were Indian like Robert, some white like us. Later, we walked through town towards a bar area looking for another drink, stepping around sleeping, staggering, screaming, fighting people.

'Lot of drunks in Prince Rupert,' said Doug to no one in particular.

'Yeah,' answered Robert with exasperation, 'mostly Indians, disappointed angry Indians.'

'Robert gets a bit pissed off with his own people,' explained one of the other men in our group.

'They're always so fucking bitter,' complained Robert.

'Yeah, well there's a lot of cultural confusion out there, not much confidence or self-respect.' It came from one of his white mates. Robert just shook his head.

The strippers in the bar were a bit clumsy, sometimes a zipper would stick, or a button catch. Some looked bored, others embarrassed. None was beautiful, but each time a piece of glittering clothing fell to the ground, or a painted hand was dragged slowly over a breast or left to linger between legs, whoops and yells filled the room. Men reached towards the stage that was all flashing lights, chrome and wetness.

I was told the story between performances. A tall black girl had just finished seducing dollars from the crowd, the music had been lowered and the patrons had settled back to drink.

Robert sipped at his Jack Daniel's before he began. He told us he was fishing for halibut in the Johnstone Strait on his boat the *Sea Eagle*, a thirty-foot hand-liner, black hull, high wheelhouse. He had anchored for the night in the channel, port and starboard lights burning, two lights on the radio mast. It was a clear evening, stars filling the sky. There was a dark edge to the night but it was far away. He saw lightning but couldn't even hear the thunder. When the boat started to lift and drop in the undetermined early morning he knew that the storm had caught them. He felt his boat nose into the wind and drift across the waves. Robert had a good anchor and a lot of chain and rope out, so he wasn't worried. He checked on deck and could only see white foam splashing on a black canvas. Nothing to do. He went back to his bunk, lay down, and a few minutes later he was flailing and choking in the cold, wild water. He could hear his deckhand screaming across the wind. He rose with the next wave and caught sight of the man clinging to a part of the *Sea Eagle*. The tanker that had sliced through their boat continued to drive straight ahead, its lights becoming dimmer, its wake adding to the confusion of the angry water. They both managed to crawl onto part of the dead boat. The storm passed. They were picked up next morning by another fishing boat, very cold and pissed off.

'No broken bones?' Doug asked in a soft respectful voice when Robert had finished.

'They kept us a day or so in Nanaimo hospital, we were almost blue,' answered Robert.

'And your boat?'

'Insurance paid up, I'm an organized Indian.'

Dixon Entrance pounded, rolled and thumped us as we headed for the Alaskan border. The thirty-five knot winds raised the water around us until we were forced to run and hide like cockroaches in a kitchen. Some days we would row five hours and make one mile. We were wet and chilled for days on end. One time when it was too rough to go out we built a large fire under a rock ledge that let you look over the frantic water but still stay dry and warm. We swelled our bellies with food, and drank cup after cup of sweet black coffee. As I smoked a long dark cigar that I had bought in Prince Rupert, Doug retrieved the shotgun out of its canvas case and started to rub grease in as a protection against rust. 'What about those waitresses at Steve's Broiler?' he suddenly asked. 'Did you sleep with any?'

Doug never talked too much about sex. Once, a little unfairly, I even asked him did he think about it. He assured me he did but always with his girl in Colorado. 'Well?' he pushed.

'Sure I did,' I finally replied.

'How many?' he asked.

'All of them,' I answered, 'Well, all except Mary.'

'Why not Mary then?'

'Strict Catholic and a grandmother.'

'And Anne from upstairs?' he continued.

'You know I did.'

'But she was only eighteen!'

'Yes, but she knew more than I did about sex.'

'And Sharon?'

'I was with her for two months.'

'Well?'

'Well nothing, I found her sleeping with another man. It didn't matter, it wouldn't have worked anyway.'

109

'But she went to Shore College, that's one of the best schools in the country, and she was beautiful.'

'Yes, she was,' I nodded.

'Have you ever thought of staying with one girl?'

'Sure, Doug, I even tried, but when they were going right I was always turning left.'

'What's that supposed to mean?' he pushed.

'Just that I haven't found one yet that's going the same way, one who wants to live the same life.'

'I think you're full of shit,' he said, rubbing more grease on the gun, 'you're never together with anybody long enough to find out, you just like fucking around. Do you know how much time you're wasting chasing all the time? You'll end up alone.'

It was not far out of Ketchikan on a finger of the Misty Fiords, before Behm Canal, early morning. The water reflected like polished wood. Flossed clouds floated by, the *Renee Blue*'s red hull mirrored itself, weaving a passage over drowned green trees that pointed downwards.

There were three jet-black dorsal fins scything through the reflections, moving in the same direction as the *Renee Blue*, parallel. It was a father, mother, baby. When you looked deeper you could clearly see the mass of the black body, the white daubing above the eye like a painted warrior, the broad flippers, the blunt nose, the white belly reaching up unevenly into the black. Masses of teeth. We thought that the killer whales were going to pass when the male turned towards us. Just before collision, he slowed, wheeled, and lay beside us, watching, his dorsal a yard higher than the gunwales, his length much greater than the *Renee Blue*. He swam with us a while, the mother and baby watching from a distance. I had seen a drawing of a killer whale taking an Eskimo from the ice, he could easily do the same to me. I was scared, but at the same time enchanted by his nearness. I could almost lean out of the *Renee Blue* and touch him. Doug assured me that they mistook the Eskimos for seals, I should not be worried, it was obvious I was not a seal. The whale had seen enough, he shot back to his family. Doug removed his glasses and wiped his itching eyes with the back of his right hand. He then placed it on my shoulder and we watched the whales silently leave.

We rowed among the boats of the Ketchikan fishing fleet looking for a moorage. Green mountains loomed at the back, shunting the town towards the water, forcing it to stretch further along the channel. The buildings had been constructed over the water on posts because that's where the commerce was, and all the room they had. Timber felled by lumbermen left the lower mountains disfigured and scarred like a wounded face. We collected our food box from the office of Northern Freighters, ate a huge meal as we always did in town, and left. Ketchikan seemed like a metropolis and we were more comfortable in the bush where we could take care of our gear and ourselves.

We spent that night in a log cabin built among tall grass and wildflowers by a hunter, or fisherman, or nature lover. There was tinned food which we did not touch. We replaced the firewood that we used to light the stove and warm the room. Mice ran about unconcerned as if they had built the place. The *Renee Blue* bobbed serenely in the protected cove. We lingered next morning, walking the pebbled beach, watching the tide, trying to decide whether to stay or leave.

The deer came down to lick salt off the rocks, it had not expected us. I waded to the boat and freed the shotgun, moved as close to the animal as I dared and fired. The cartridge caught her in the flank, she fell crippled, turned her head to look at me, her large brown eyes in panic. I raced towards her, ejected the empty cartridge, ejected the next which was birdshot, and fired the third into her head, crushing it, killing her quickly.

I had never skinned a deer.

'Can't be too much different than a kangaroo,' Doug encouraged me. I started from the back hoof, slitting the heel and working up, hand ripping the skin as I cut. When all four feet were done I gutted her, joining the cut to the legs and peeling the skin off her body. The head I severed with a machete. It was a rough job but I had saved most of the meat, the heart and liver were laid on a rock ready for immediate frying. Doug, who made fires as he did all other things – slowly, precisely – started gathering small, larger and still larger twigs. He fashioned them into a tepee, small twigs first, blew to make sure there was enough oxygen, then carefully built up the heat by adding new fuel until the fire ate upon itself and roared. All the wood was damp. I tied rope around the deer's skinless back legs, hoisted the rope over a branch and hung her to bleed. Later we salted her with coarse salt that we had brought along for that purpose. We ate the liver and heart slowly, chewing each mouthful, letting their juices wash around our mouths before swallowing.

The current in the middle of the channel ran strong and pulled the light aluminium boat tight against its anchor line. As we rowed closer we could see that it was piled high with empty traps. There were no oars. Small bubbles appeared around the motor shaft, soon a head appeared covered with goggles and a snorkel. A sandy-haired diver threw a rubber-handled knife into the back of the boat before hoisting himself over the edge, landing, sitting in one motion on the seat closest to the motor. He hadn't seen us. As he reefed at his mask, he twisted and caught sight of us, a smile filled his smooth face. 'Geez, who are you guys?'

The diver's name was Todd, his motor had been snarled with

floating rope. Todd was a lightly built, fifteen-year-old crab fisherman. He was working alone. We were fifty miles out of Ketchikan and forty before Wrangell with nothing in between except water and bush.

As he towed us back to his camp, which turned out to be a large canvas tent set up on flattened scrub on the inner lip of a small cove, he explained that he had been working with three other men but they found it too lonely and had returned with the boat that comes to pick up the catch.

'It's a pigsty,' apologized Todd as we carried our gear up from the boat. I looked around: the tent was large, four cot beds, a gas refrigerator, a fold-up table. Clothes littered the canvas floor, half-eaten foods covered the table, filthy dishes were piled high in a bucket near the entrance, garbage had been thrown together in a pile, traps lay strewn about outside. Todd told us that at night, black bears came down to the edge of the light thrown out by the kerosene lamps. Seduced by the filth, I thought. Todd kept a 30.06 hunting rifle upright by the entrance in case they came further. That evening we washed a few dishes, boiled crab and fried deer steak and shrimp on his gas stove and sipped the whisky that I had bought in Ketchikan.

Todd told us that he was born in Wrangell. His light blue eyes and pale skin colour suggested, like so many inhabitants of the area, a Scandinavian history. When I asked him about his work he seemed surprised.

'Just working my school vacation,' he answered shyly.

'Yeah,' replied Doug, 'but most kids wash cars or cut lawns for extra money. I worked at a 7-Eleven.'

Todd didn't seem to understand the compliment. 'My girl might come down the next time they collect the crab,' he happily told us, 'guess I got to clean the place up a bit.'

Before we left next morning we watched Todd pull traps,

straining with the effort, hand over hand, alone, the current rushing by. Then we slowly rowed away.

The next few days we gorged ourselves on deer. We had left a big piece with Todd and wanted to finish the rest before it began to rot. Each evening, because it had rained and the wood was wet, Doug with his infinite patience lit the fire, and the deer was fried and eaten with dumplings. Afterwards it was built up until it burned away the dampness that seemed to be constantly with us now, and we would lie back on logs counting the stars in the clearness between the dark travelling clouds. One evening Doug pulled out the fishing line, sat on a rock in the drizzle and fought a small salmon. Next day we gave what was left of the deer to a passing fisherman, we could not finish all of her. It had been six days since I had shot her on the beach.

I had read that Wrangell began as a fur-trading settlement. Otter, seal, mink and lynx were traded by the Tlingit Indians. It had been settled by the Russians, the English and Americans, but those days are long past. As we rowed in, a large Japanese freighter that had come to collect lumber from the mills stood under cranes that were readying to load her. Tugboats, seaplanes and seine trawlers filled the moorings and salmon and shrimp canneries worked noisily along the waterfront.

It had started to rain heavily, incessantly, and we had started to argue pretty well all the time. We were nearing the end of the trip and it had begun to resemble a marriage breaking down. All we remembered were the difficult parts, all we recognized in each other were the annoying things. We were meant to row into Wrangell quietly, unnoticed, buy tobacco and leave. There was no need to linger, we had no money to buy a bed, but I wanted to drink, I needed company. Doug never needed it, he hardly ever spoke. Along with the tobacco, I bought whisky. We left still arguing.

If you look to starboard as you row out of Wrangell, not forgetting that as a rower you are facing the back of the boat, you would see a great mass of brown-coloured water. It is river water pushing silt and mud out into the tideline. Brown churning into aqua-green. Where it slows, there's bound to be fine gold but it's almost impossible to retrieve. The river is the Stikine and its gold is carried down from upper British Columbia four hundred miles away. It was along this river that Americans travelled into British Columbia in the latter part of the nineteenth century to make their fortune; it was because of this river that Wrangell ceased to be just a fur-trading outpost.

Towards Petersburg, reaching closer and closer to Juneau, arguing more and more. The rain pounded down. I asked Doug once if anything I did annoyed him, 'You never rinse the soap off the dishes,' he replied immediately.

Knife-sharp peaks stood at a distance looking over the neatness and bustle of a town built on muskeg meadows by Scandinavians and known as Little Norway. Petersburg is a fishing town. A passage of water known as Wrangell Narrows fronts the town. Twenty miles of tricky navigation, marked with coloured lights, flashing beacons and bobbing red buoys that point out the danger. Fishing boats, tugs and tankers bunched up trying to get through. We rowed along ignoring the warnings, safe with our shallow draught and self-propulsion. We never visited Petersburg, we were pulled by the fever of arriving at the end.

In Frederick Sound small blue-white, white-blue shapes of ice floated around on the feisty little waves, reminding you of young girls in ball frocks dancing and curtsying. Whales flew high out of the water ahead of us, fell back, pounding the sea, dived deep, turned and shot again towards the sky, and again fell. Spray surged upwards spreading like a glass curtain. The sun burned through making colours. As we came closer we saw that they were humpback whales, black and thick, fifty foot long, a pod, they were feeding in a circle, mouths open. We sat drifting in the *Renee Blue*, watching the frenzied feeding, the cliffs of water, marvelling at the power needed to propel the heavy mass so high. Doug used a strip of plastic as a cover against rain, set our small gas cooker underneath, primed and lit it, and then started boiling coffee water. He pulled out his chewing tobacco, lay back against the side of the dory, let one hand fall soaking into the sea, and with the other began to fill his mouth, never taking his eyes from the whales. I brewed and poured the coffee, lit a cigar and did the same.

'I've decided to stay in Alaska,' Doug suddenly, unexpectedly told me, still mesmerized by the spectacle. The light wind burned my cigar ash a fierce red, the rain made it soft and spongy.

As we rowed along the last part of Stephens Passage, the wind stinging our backs, the rainwater filling the boat, nearing Juneau with every stroke, I understood completely, that it was over. I felt a sudden, unreasonable pride, and then later, anxiety, and still later, a deep nostalgic sadness. Feelings I recognized that come with the end of something, before a beginning.

We had been living together more than six months. All our thoughts, our energies, our money had gone towards the trip. We had rowed through daunting beauty, wild, breathtaking country, and because of our noiseless, slow progress, we had come closer to animals than we had thought possible. We had drifted on seas so calm that they could have been ponds in a backyard, and suffered through weather that made rowing so heavy it left our bodies burning with pain. We had run low on food and on tobacco. The last month we had woken only to morning cold and rain that soaked our humour and made uncramping our hands almost impossible. Tension had run high, insults were spat out without thought, but just once did we almost start swinging, and then only because exhaustion and frustration had smothered anything resembling good sense. And now it was over.

We rowed under the metal coat-hanger bridge that joins Juneau to Douglas, and tied up among the small fishing fleet. It was raining. It had taken us four and a half months of preparation, and two and a half months of rowing. In the end we understood that it had nothing to do with old-time gold miners heading north, it was only about doing something.

The trip had strong, opposite effects on both of us. I saw it as a beginning, the first cold beer on a hot Friday night after a week of hard work. It became my catalyst to a sometimes unreasonable need to see strange places, and do different things. My life would never be settled again. For Doug it was the end. A magnificent, frivolous taste of adventure. When we reached Juneau he decided that that was enough. Life must now become uncomplicated, conventional, settled. We both understood that it was the end of our time together, for always.

I found a job on a salmon-fishing boat, and returned to Australia three months later. Doug worked for a while in a fish processing plant, and then moved to Anchorage, where as far as I know he still lives. For months afterwards I would have to knead my fingers to start them working in the mornings, for years afterwards beer glasses would drop without warning through my hand and crash, spilling glass and precious liquid around the feet of my drinking pals. They would never believe it had nothing to do with drunkenness, but came from rowing a boat to Alaska.

THE *ALASKA SHARK*

Two snow-capped mountains stand at the back of Juneau, Alaska, hemming it in against Gastineau Channel, which is just a finger of the sea. Behind those mountains there is an ice-field and more mountains, and then more. The town climbs into the toes of these mountains, gives up and returns to the sea, tries again, and again gives up, and so on.

The weather in Juneau can be inclement. During the summer months the sun lingers but is often forced to fight its way through deep, grey, wind-ripped clouds. In the winter, when the sun hangs low, clouds come down and touch the rooftops dropping freezing rain, leaving you numb with cold. In Juneau you can be stung by gales that push snow and sleet through the narrow streets at a pace that leaves a whistle in the air. Ice can gather on the roads making walking difficult, or hang like daggers from balconies and eaves leaving it dangerous to linger. At times like these, people need a place to be warm and hidden. Mine was a bar on the main street called The Red Dog Saloon.

The Dog, as everybody called it, had a wooden floor covered with sawdust; you made a swishing sound as you moved about. The heads of a growling bear, a massive-antlered deer and a bearded goat decorated the walls. Half of a large moose had been mounted behind the bar. On this evening the round wooden tables were filled with loggers who had come down from their bush camps to drink up a storm. Men made rough and coarse by isolation, and hardened by their work in the hills amongst the tallest timber in the world. An unkempt and smiling hermit sat slurping beer and chattering away to anybody who would listen. There was a smattering of tourists trying to feel Alaskan, a few government workers because Juneau was the state capital, and there were fishermen.

I was sitting with the crew of the *Nelly O'Hara*, a purse-seiner, sipping two-dollar Budweiser beer when he came in.

'I need a deckhand to work on a hand trawler, if anybody asks.' It was a heavy man who spoke in a loud wind-chipped voice to the barmaid. He wore a coarse woollen shirt, a full beard, and braces to hold his woollen pants, as did most Alaskans. I turned enquiringly to Cheryl, the skipper of the *Nelly O'Hara*.

'He's a fair man,' she said to me, anticipating my question, 'and he's got a good boat. I'm just sorry I've got a full crew or I would take you on,' she continued, grabbing my leg on my inside thigh and moving her hand upwards until it rested on my crotch. 'But that's OK,' she continued, 'we've still got tonight.'

I became hard, and then curious. 'Why me?' I asked. 'There's fifty men to one woman in Alaska, you can take your pick.'

She smiled and drew on a cigarette before she answered, 'I like small blond men with blue eyes and funny accents. But don't go feeling too proud, I don't want to marry you.'

'I need work and I work hard,' I said, moving to stand beside him.

'It's the end of the season,' he told me, 'you won't make much money. Can you cook?' he demanded.

119

'No,' I answered truthfully.

'Well let's hope you can pull up the anchor. The last man I had couldn't even do that. Be on the docks at six tomorrow morning, the boat's called *Alaska Shark*.'

'I didn't know there was one.'

'There ain't,' he answered roughly.

The dock was too small for the seiners, hand-liners and fishing skiffs that lay next to each other like poor children sharing a bed. When the weather was fine they floated unmoving and dignified on water that was polished green-blue ice, but when the weather turned bad the wind would race up the channel, chipping at the water, turning it back on itself, pushing the boats against each other, scraping paint and tearing metal and, if your boat was made from wood, rasping away pieces that could create fatal leaks.

I stood waiting for my boss on the dock in the early morning. It was clear and fresh with just the slightest breeze rippling the water. A mist sat amongst the trees on the far side of the channel. The sun that had only just begun to struggle over the mountains to the east, touched the ice-field creating a pink layer of light, hemming the morning greyness.

The *Alaska Shark* was tied to the far side of a large black-hulled seiner. As we climbed across the fishing boat, we had to step around nets, over buckets, buoys and ropes that lay strewn about like toys in a child's playpen.

'Put the food below,' ordered the captain, whose name I had just learned was Dave.

I climbed down into a space so small it left you looking for room to turn. On my left was a two-burner gas cooker and next to that a large gas bottle. The cooker was resting on a food cupboard. A half-sized fridge that was powered by the boat batteries stood next to it. Above the stove was another cupboard where the cracked plates and chipped mugs were kept; that's where I was told to store the brandy bottles that would become a part of our nightly ritual.

On the other side was a small table, our eating place in bad weather. Forward of the kitchen, in the nose of the boat, was the sleeping area. Two bunks opposite each other, and built over storage boxes that held ropes, lanterns, fishing tackle, extra knives, and flotation devices. You don't really need them, I learned later, because even in September the water was cold enough to kill you before you drowned, but it was regulations.

I walked back through the boat and up the two stairs to the wheelhouse that was just a half roof covering the wheel, and found Dave in the bowels of the boat pumping out bilge that smelled like high octane vomit.

'Make some coffee. What did you say your name was?'

'Macca,' I called back. 'Macca.'

The engine started on the second turn. I raced up onto the deck to cast us off. As we moved away from the black-hulled seiner, the water churned by our propeller caused her to bang lightly against the dock.

The *Alaska Shark* headed south-east along the channel, past the town that was born of gold fever and matured with fishing, timber and government, past the old disused mine face that gaped at you from the mountain like the mouth of a sad dead thing. Past the landfill that was the entrails of the old mine, and out into Stephens Passage on the north side of Admiralty Island, heading steadily for the fishing grounds near the open sea.

'Take the wheel, will ya? Keep it on that heading and we shouldn't hit anything. And if we pass another boat turn her into the wake, that way we won't tip over if it's big.'

'She tips over easy then does she?' I asked, concerned.

'It's a bloody cork, a big cork. You ever fished before, Macca? Did I say that right?'

'Yeah, you got it. No.'

'You'll learn.' We sipped our coffee slowly, getting to know each other quietly.

The *Alaska Shark* pushed steadily along on the late summer day on water that playfully skipped and hopped in the wind that drifted along the passage. She wove into the wakes made by bigger boats, taking them head on, untroubled.

'How did you get to Alaska, Macca?'

'I rowed a boat up here, a Grand Banks dory.'

'Ain't that a little dangerous?'

'No, you can't sink a dory, it was just hard work.'

'Where did you come from?'

'Seattle,' I answered.

'You rowed a boat a thousand miles?'

'Me and a mate.'

'Well then I suppose you'll be able to lift the anchor at least.'

The first thing we noticed were the jet-black dorsal fins slicing the surface of the water like an electric hand saw cutting into sun-dried pine. They raced to meet us as we chugged sluggishly towards them. Soon you could see the white patches over their eyes, and count the fins, some so big that you couldn't imagine the size of the body they were piloting, others so small you knew a strong man could hold the animal in his arms. A pack of twenty-two killer whales drove at our boat and then split into two groups before impact. They passed on either side, enjoying their game, rolling the *Alaska Shark* this way and that.

As they passed we caught glimpses of white underbelly as it crept up the back side of the whale, eating away the borders of the black like a bad finger-painting. I stood watching their dorsal fins getting smaller and smaller, melting into the late afternoon shadows.

'Jesus,' I gasped.

'Some sight eh, got them where you come from?'

'No mate, what do they eat?'

'Oh, other whales, sea lions, seals, fish, you, me.'

We arrived at the fishing grounds on Icy Strait just before the light turned dark enough to blind us to the offshore rocks that dotted the coast like sea lions basking in the sun. Silhouettes of boats, some tied together in little communities, could be seen bobbing gently up and down in the dying light. The thickly forested shoreline that seemed to grow into the water loomed black.

Dave, who had been content to let me do all the driving, took the wheel from me and guided the *Shark* into a gash in the land. A rocky shoreline on three sides. 'When I say so, get that anchor over the side, and keep your feet away from the rope. Wouldn't want you getting dragged into the sea and ending up fish bait the first night.' Dave manoeuvred carefully, watching the depth finder and checking his charts at the same time. On his call, I squatted down and heaved the anchor from the deck, dropping it carefully onto the mirror of water, splintering it into a million shards.

'Good,' yelled Dave, 'you can lift a dry anchor, let's see you pull it out of the mud tomorrow.'

The weather was soft. The light breeze that blew was still a child of summer. The sky was wide, star filled. The water glowed with the phosphorescent darting of fish around the sleeping boat.

The first night we ate simply: fried eggs and coffee on the deck under the moon. After the meal Dave brought out the brandy which we sipped while checking the line that was rolled around a spool, hooked and ready. Our iceboxes were filled with clean white ice: a fishing boat's morgue. Before we slept we smoked a joint together.

At first the anchor didn't move. I dropped my grip lower, turned my shoulders in and heaved again, nothing, Dave had already started the motor. It idled, sounding rough, coughing a little. The seagulls that dived around the fishing fleet screeched in annoyance. Again I heaved: this time it moved. I turned a little to see if Dave had been watching. I didn't see him. One hand over the other, knees bent a little, straining on every pull. At last it broke free of the water. The wrestle to drag the mud-embalmed piece of iron over the side of the boat left me panting. I squatted, weak.

'Heavy mother, ain't it?' Dave called from the galley where he had been making coffee. 'Clean that mud off will ya, Macca?'

While the sun yawned and stretched, we moved out to fish, baiting the hooks and reeling out as we motored. The *Alaska Shark* had four spools of line, two on either side towards the back of the boat. A hand winch turned the spools, letting line in and out. The line ran through pulleys that were attached to a bent steel rod ahead of the spools: these kept the lines running smoothly. We stood in a deep well below the spools to gaff the salmon off the line, without the danger of them flipping back over the side of the boat and escaping. Undersized salmon and un-sellable catch were always thrown back.

We fished in the Icy Strait, an eyelash of the Pacific between Chicago Island and the mainland in a procession of hardy little hand-liners called *Sahara*, *Mary*, *Ginny* and *Rusty*. Nose to tail, nose to tail, following one another like elephants in a circus parade.

'Makes you sick having to fish in a crowd, but we've got no choice. The fisheries department tells you where you can fish and for how long. This time it's Icy Strait for four days. The fish are running here at the moment, that's why there are so many boats.'

We motored on an oval course hoping to hook the fish the others missed.

'Keep checking the land,' Dave advised, 'without knowing it you can drift in and end up on the rocks. And watch the silly bastards ahead of you real good.'

Around and around we drove, hour after hour, passing over the same water, the same forest. Citadels of hemlock and spruce. Fierce-looking bald eagles perched, watching us go past with arched necks and tigers' eyes. Seagulls swarmed around our riggings hoping for an easy meal.

Boats would greet each other as they passed, messages would be yelled back and forth, questions would be asked about catches, lies would be told. You pissed in a bucket because many of the other skippers were women.

'The women I know couldn't care less,' Dave told me the first morning. 'Hell, they would prefer to piss over the side of the boat.'

'Then what's the problem?' I asked.

'Good old-fashioned US morals I suppose, that's just the way we do it.' We drank coffee and more coffee, bullshitted, and watched the lines pulling heavier, straining with bright, shiny salmon.

'Get them in, Macca. Let's kill some fish.' I turned the handle on the winch, setting my back and straining with the weight. Dave kept the *Shark* running, not letting the lines drop.

As the first one neared I gaffed it under the gills, hauling it over the side, and then the next and the next. I set the lock on the winch, turned my gaff hook around and used it as a club, bringing it down on heads of salmon that flipped and jumped. Only then could I remove the hooks.

The salmon were mostly coho, but sometimes we would pull in a king, or a pink. Large, handsome, sparkling clean. They were returning to their birth streams to spawn. Now they lay dying, their deep black pupils shocked and sightless, blood running from their mouths and the wounds on their heads, smudging and staining their silver beauty. But they would be cleaned and dressed, and look as good lying in a tray of ice at a fishmonger's as they did swimming freely in life.

Around and around we ran, winching, clubbing, re-baiting, icing the catch, following the other boats like dogs after a bitch on heat.

There was no warning unless you were looking closely at the exact spot that it came from. Then you may have seen a disturbance in the water, a small turbulence. But for those who were busy with other things you noticed nothing until the whale broke the surface, speared skywards as straight as an engine-driven rocket, and then fell back to the sea, bursting it apart, sending heavy waves punching in all directions. Spray flecked the sky, caught the wind, and drenched you.

'That's a humpback,' yelled Dave, jumping up from his resting position against the spools at the back of the *Shark*. 'Fifty foot long – ain't she beautiful?'

The whale had sounded four metres off the bow of the *Debora*, a boat that had anchored out of the fishing lane with engine trouble. Its skipper, a short, heavy, bearded man, was standing on the bow when the whale breached. Up went his arms in terror, backwards he moved, further backwards, until he fell sprawling over his own ropes in terror. The bells and sirens of the fleet were still sounding in tribute to the great spectacle when the whale came again. So slowly did she seem to rise the second time that you could count some of the plates on the upper jaw. Sea fell from the thick-bodied animal like water over a fall. The massive flukes slapped powerfully down on the sea.

We ran the *Alaska Shark* fourteen hours a day, and every evening we anchored as Dave wished, alone and at peace. My job was to check that the fish were iced, clean the blood and guts from the well, wash down the decks, check the lines and hooks, grease the winch, and shape the ship. Dave would cook and complain about it like a child who wanted all the toys in the toy box.

We ate on the deck under the sky and drank our coffee with a brandy. We always finished by sharing a joint.

'A lot of people smoke up here?' I asked the first night.

'Most of the fleet I'd say,' he replied before dragging deeply and holding his breath till his face reddened and he began to spit.

'It's goddamn legal in Alaska,' he shouted out, using the last of his exhaling breath. 'She's a hell of a state.'

Dave talked in spurts. His stories seemed to take forever. He would start and stop, change subject, begin anew, or just stop talking. Sometimes after our brandy, as we smoked, he would just lie back, saying nothing, and adore the stars that seemed so close you could almost pull them down and hide them in your pockets. But not all the time.

'You ever hunted, Macca?' he asked, near the end of the first joint on the first evening, when my body was beaten and I was too tired to think. 'Yeah, a bit,' I yawned. 'Roos when I was young, rabbits, some wild pigs. Since I've been up here, I've shot a few deer.'

'Do you know, an Alaskan brown bear can grow eight feet tall and weigh fifteen hundred pounds. You see them fishing salmon and they remind you of a pup playing with a ball. All big, furry and occupied.

'A few years ago I had a job as a guide, a bear killing guide. It's pretty strictly controlled,' he explained when he saw the surprised look on my face. 'There's a quota, they're not going to let you wipe out the whole bear population. I worked for a boss who owned a white fifty-two-foot cruiser, wood panelling, state-of-the-art galley, a full liquor cabinet. His clients would pay five thousand dollars to hunt bear. They came from Maine, New York, hell from everywhere. In the mornings it was bear time. We hunted a lot around Admiralty Island. It's ninety-six miles long, good sheltered bays and plenty of coastal brown bear. They're the biggest, a lot bigger than grizzly. They have better food, a lot of plant life, berries, small black-tail deer, and salmon. They grow massive.'

Dave stopped his story as suddenly as he had begun, yawned, touched my shoulder, and reminded me I had to get that anchor up in the morning. As I headed down into the cabin I looked a last time to the empty rocky shore that seemed too close. And then up to the tree tops that were swaying delicately in the breeze, waving goodnight.

The wind picked up in the night. Cold grey clouds formed, and we had to fight against a rising sea all the next day. It became more difficult to handle the boat, which was being pushed sideways by the swell. Winching became heavier as the waves fought the incoming fish. Still we pulled in salmon, pulled in money. In the evening we found that the wind had snuck into our cove. The *Alaska Shark* bounced around a little as we ate our food, drank our coffee and brandy, as we shared the nightly joint. You had to wedge yourself against the icebox to stop yourself from toppling over.

Dave pulled his collar up against the breeze and began, 'Anyway, this one time.'

'What are you talking about?' I asked.

'The bear story I started last night, Macca, concentrate. You had too much to smoke? Anyway, I was guiding a guy from Connecticut, a lawyer, knew fuck all about the woods. Just had plenty of money and wanted a head to put on his wall.'

'Did that worry you, that he knew nothing?' I asked staring at the water. 'He was paying you a lot of money.'

'Yeah,' answered Dave, 'I know it doesn't make sense but I read something when I was a kid about the Bushmen of the Kalahari apologizing to the animal before they killed it. The least we could do before we killed was to know a little about where he lives and how. Show it some kind of respect. But I guess nobody has time any more.

'Anyway, we moved up to the edge of a muskeg bog and squatted beside a large red spruce. The tree line was thick right to the wet. There was fog, but it had risen and floated into the tops of the trees leaving our view clear. A large cedar had fallen and lay drowning in the bog. We heard a low grunt. Then we saw her. A brown, staring at us but not seeing. Bears have bad eyesight.

'She lifted her head above the log, and her shoulders followed. She was young and big. I called gently to the lawyer. "There she is," I said, motioning with the barrel of my rifle.

'The bear sensed something was wrong, she rose a little, sniffed, dropped back down, and then rose again. 'Fire, man, fire,' I whispered. Nothing – he was too nervous. The bear growled deeply from her belly and stood to her full height.

'We were well hidden and upwind – she couldn't smell us. She dropped back down and then started pawing over the log in our direction. I fired, she dropped back and disappeared. I waited, the lawyer was still squatting, staring at the ground. I had a clear chest shot – she should have been dead but then her head appeared again over the log. I fired a second time. She dropped. All we could see was the drowning tree with its massive roots still covered in dirt and its branches that were still thick with grey foliage. I waited, again she came, this time rising in profile. Her colour seemed different, the hump larger. I brought my rifle to my shoulder and fired a third time. I caught her clean, you could see the bullet hit the fur, explode. Down she went again.

'I was using a .306 caliber – it can kill anything. I waited five minutes before I started sloshing alone through the bog towards the cedar. There were three dead bears. The first bear's nose lay buried in the bog, its left paw caught amongst the branches, a puncture had opened his chest over the heart. The second had fallen on top of the first, its mouth had pulled all the way back over its teeth. It was a lighter shade of brown. They were both matted with mud and looked like rugs laid out to be beaten. The third I could now clearly see was much larger with a yellowish coat.'

Dave breathed deeply and continued. 'Fine white hairs tipped her back, making me think of a very fat middle-aged lady I once knew. There was a nauseating stink of wet fur, bog mud and blood around them. I had shot three bears, a mother and two, almost full-grown cubs. Give up hunting, Macca, that's my advice, we've got no right to kill.'

'What about fish?' I coughed, sucking the marijuana deeply down my throat.

'That's different, you don't feel for fish. Besides, I got to make a living. Maybe you want me to cut down trees? Let's get some sleep.'

By the next morning the wind was howling down the Icy Strait. Some of the fleet was out but many had stayed anchored, warm and safe. We had been fishing for an hour, rolling and shaking with the churned sea, when Dave, who had been in the cabin checking his charts, stuck his head through the galley hatch. 'Macca, fuck this, the fish are seasick, they're not going to bite. Winch in the lines, I'll take the wheel, we're heading across the channel where we can get some cover from the wind.'

It took us two hours of motoring through sea that I thought would splinter us any second. I had been below resting at the beginning of the crossing, but kept banging my head on the bottom side of the deck each time we crossed over a wave and dipped into the trough. I started imagining the water bursting through the bow, filling the cabin with cold salt seasoned water. Deck was a better place for me.

'I'll take over, Dave, get some rest.'

And without a care in the world he gave me a heading and ducked below to sleep.

When we arrived on the north side of Chicago straits, the wind was coming out of the north.

'Head her east around the point,' I was ordered as we hugged into the land trying to block the wind. The tide was performing its six hourly turnaround, and in Alaska, where you have twenty-feet tide differences, that meant a lot of water rushing in and rushing out. A rip tide was building on the point, whirlpools had formed, and with the storm whipping and mixing, the water was a bubbling cauldron. The *Shark* became unbalanced like a man on a three-day drunk. Stumbling forward, sideways, twisting. The motor pushed us ever so slowly forward against waves that were breaking full over the cabin.

Suddenly we started rolling like we were going right over ourselves. Dave screamed at me that a stabilizing arm had become twisted in the radio mast. 'Get up and untangle it,' he yelled. I climbed to the roof of the cabin, then part way up the mast and started tugging, pushing and yanking, but with more concern for staying on the boat than for the job I was doing. 'Dave, the bastard won't move,' I called back down to him. Up he came, fuming and swearing, 'Take the fucking wheel and try to keep us off the rocks.' Dave untwisted it in a few minutes, and in a few minutes more we were around the point and turning into a small bay that had been water-weathered out of the high cliffs.

The opening was just wide enough to get the *Shark* through, but once inside we found it to be oval in shape, and large enough to anchor a small fleet. Its surface was green and docile, and it was surrounded by tree-lined cliffs giving it the appearance of a dormant baby volcano. Not a wisp of breeze ruffled the water. I had just got the anchor down when Dave came to stand beside me. 'Sorry I yelled at you back there, I guess I was just worried about my boat.'

'That's all right,' I answered, 'I was so scared I didn't notice. What do we do now?'

Dave went below and came back with the brandy. 'That's what we do.'

We had taken a sip from our first glass when an open launch came scuttling through the opening. A lone man at the rudder. 'Did you see my uncle?' he yelled up at us from his twenty-foot boat.

'Come aboard,' called Dave.'

'It's my uncle,' he repeated as he scrambled up. When he pulled down the hood of his rain gear, I saw a broad brown face, long dark hair and almond eyes. 'He went fishing and never came back.'

'Give him a drink, Macca, what's your name?'

'James,' he softly answered, 'James Thomas.'

'I'll get on the radio, James. What sort of boat is he in?' Dave asked back over his shoulder as he moved below to call.

'Same as mine, a launch. It's called *Candy*, supposed to be around here somewhere.'

'Where are you from, mate?' I asked, trying to calm him a little.

'Hoonah, a village about five miles east of here. Just inside Port Fredrick, I'm a Tlingit.'

Dave put out his call for information but without luck. James sipped the brandy but did so walking up to Dave, back to me, up to Dave.

'Well?' I finally asked.

'Get the anchor up, Macca, we have to go and look. A skiff won't last long in this weather.'

'James,' I called, 'give us a hand with this bloody monster.'

We had her halfway over the side of the boat when a message came in from Hoonah. James's uncle had just arrived. He was safe.

'I'm not unhappy about that radio call, Dave.'

'Neither am I, Macca. In this weather I wasn't looking forward to that at all, not at all. Let's have a drink.'

'Tell me about being a Tlingit, Jimmy.'

Jimmy looked at Dave to make sure I was serious.

'He just got here, Jimmy, and he comes from the other side of the world, he don't know much about your people.'

Jimmy seemed pacified. 'It's the name of an Indian nation, my nation. We are hunters and fishers. The two major ones in this part of Alaska are the Tlingit and Haida. But we're more powerful.'

I nodded, wondering what the Haida people I had met on my rowing trip would think about that.

In the four hours that James stayed with us we finished a bottle of brandy, soaking it up with fried fish cooked in butter and served with stale bread. We were careful with each other in the beginning, our conversation full of mutual respect. James explained the Tlingit custom of recording important events on totem poles. I described the habits of kangaroos and koalas. But it wasn't long before the brandy inspired a comradely intimacy and our talk turned to the sexual delights of Tlingit girls compared to Australian girls, and then American girls. Our laughter echoed around the *Shark* like the screams of the insane.

In the late afternoon the wind died down and with much thanks James sped off through the gap in the cliffs, heading for Hoonah. A loud quiet came over us, Dave poured another brandy. The dark grey clouds pulled the night down on top of the *Alaska Shark*.

'A good bloke,' I said, rousing myself from the melancholy that often comes after the party is over.

'We'll see him tomorrow,' mumbled Dave a little drunkenly, 'we need gas.'

We pulled up to a wharf built high on pylons to cope with the tides. Fishing seiners waiting out the dying breaths of the storm, floated snugly together in the bay.

Hoonah is laid out in rows. Its wooden houses are built high off the ground and back from the water line. They nudge at the forest edge. Dressed mostly in flaking paint, they seem sad and resigned, like old people who know their best days are past.

'What do they do here, Dave?'

'Oh, fishing. They process crabs, fish, all sorts of seafood. Or they drink. A lot of drinking.'

It was low tide when we arrived and an unsmiling man in a red plaid shirt lowered the gasoline hose down to us. We had to climb a high vertical ladder to reach the dock, in order to pay the man. It was still early as we stood looking down over the small harbour, dull green under the wispy grey clouds. The only other people about were the village fishermen standing in groups, staring down at their boats, watching the weather, trying to decide if it was worth it to go out on the last day. James stood in one group, head bowed, saying something to one of the other men.

'James, g'day James,' I called. James looked up, smiled shyly, nodded, and then dropped his head and continued talking.

'What sort of welcome is that, Dave?' I asked as we walked to the end of the wharf heading for town. 'We had a bloody good drink together yesterday, a good time. We were going out after his uncle and then he treats you like you're a woman he slept with and is ashamed of.'

'That's about right, Macca. In front of his own people he ain't gunna make a big fuss. It's a sort of new cultural awareness. You know, I'm an Indian and you're the whites that stole my land, my heritage.'

'Is that the way it was, Dave?'

'Well, we never warred against them, we just sort of moved in like bad relations and never left. Swallowed them up, made their Indian way of living obsolete. Doesn't leave a man much. Just a lot of time on his hands, and time and anger ain't much of a life.'

'Yeah, but not speaking to you after the good time we had, that's bullshit.'

134

'Yeah, I know, but it ain't the same with everybody. Let's buy some food.'

We walked slowly along a dirt road that ran along the back of the houses towards the shop. An old couple sat on their back stairs breathing in the morning, talking with each other. They nodded as we passed. A drunk man sat with his back to an electricity pole staring at the ground. A mother walked with her small son stepping around the puddles that decorated the road.

The general store was just that: the tinned food was stacked right alongside the hooks and fishing line, which was right next to the bread, which was beside the saws and hammers. Sweets stood on the counter in glass jars, cigarettes and chewing tobacco were out of reach behind the cash register. The old lady who served us was unhurried and friendly.

We bought some bread and bacon to vary our diet, and cigarettes because ours had become wet during the storm. As we turned to leave, two men and a woman entered the store. The woman, dressed in a knee-length black dress and dark stockings, seemed out of place amongst the gaily-coloured goods that were sold in the shop. The men wore plaid woollen shirts and jeans like most people, but worn with a fastidiousness that warned you they were different. All three were smiling widely, a practised grin, one you had to train your muscles to hold.

'Who were they?' I asked after we had passed, surprised at seeing other white people in Hoonah.

'Christians, fucking holier-than-thou born-agains. You know the type, you're either one of them or you've got no-good sitting on your shoulder. They've got property up at Game Creek, it's about five miles from here by boat.'

'Do they keep to themselves?'

'Fuck no, people who think they're cleaner than everybody else never stick to themselves. Every chance they get they'll be preaching. A lot of Hoonah people are churchgoers anyway, the Presbyterians got here a hundred years ago, but that's not good enough for these born-agains. You know, James is probably right to ignore us, we always fuck them up in the end. Let's go fishing, Macca.'

We anchored for the last evening again in the small bay with the tree-lined cliffs. The sky had cleared completely and left a dazzling display of silver on black. Dave sat very quietly. It had not been a successful trip. He would make very little and I would make less, but that was the risk of fishing. Next time it might be better.

'Are you going to smoke all of that marijuana, Macca? Up here in Alaska we share it.'

'What?' I asked, not taking my eyes off the sky.

'The joint,' he repeated.

'Oh yeah, sorry mate.'

It was our second smoke that evening, a sort of celebration because it would be our last night on the water, and I was feeling numb.

'What are you looking at?'

'That light keeps moving.'

Dave squinted, following the direction of my pointing finger. 'It is moving, yeah, it's moving.'

Ever so slowly it grew, still heading directly towards us.

'You believe in UFOs, Macca? They see them a lot up here, people have been taken.'

'Sure, Dave, sometimes I think you're a spaceman.'

'Well laugh if you want, but it's the truth.' The lights were starting to take a round form now, still heading directly for the *Shark*, coming closer and closer. Dave suddenly sprang to his feet.

'They're coming, Macca, they're coming.'

The lights dipped suddenly as if they had just noticed us. Down they came, and further down. Dave took off towards the back of the icebox, fell, got up, slipped, made it, and crouched down.

'Fuck,' I screamed to no one in particular, his panic becoming mine as they continued coming downwards, getting nearer. I retreated, almost knocking Dave sprawling as I snuggled in beside him behind the box. The lights were on top of us now, blinking and flashing, but when all hope had gone they suddenly became part of something else, something recognizable: a single-engine Cessna screamed at us directly above. Its shadow covered the *Alaska Shark*.

'Dave,' I whispered, 'do you want a toke?'

'Thanks, Macca.'

Where are they flying to, Dave?'

'Hoonah's got a gravel runway now, I suppose we're on its landing path.'

'Funny time to be flying.'

'Yeah, we usually only get UFOs this time of night . . .'

Back in Juneau we tied up just past the *Nelly O'Hara*. Most of the fleet had already returned. It was dark, but calm. Just the gentlest of breezes blowing out of the mountains.

'We unload at six in the morning, Macca, don't be late,' Dave reminded me as we stepped onto the badly lit floating walkways and began our stiff-legged trip to the shore. The boats banged rhythmically against the dock as we passed, reminding us not to forget them.

'A couple at The Dog?' I asked as we climbed the last few yards to solid ground. Dave turned to me, smiled, and nodded.

JUAN BRAVOS

We were looking for gold, working in Piedras Blancas, a mountainous jungle area where the rivers began, before they trickled, rushed, and bullied their way to the level of the sea where they became fat and old, flowing towards death. Antonio was my partner, or I was his. He had been gold mining for twenty years; I had just begun. We had met in a bar, built next to a dusty road, beside a small inlet on the coast. He spoke in English to me, I spoke no Spanish. We drank together, or rather I drank; Antonio sipped Coca-Cola. 'I believe in Jesus,' he explained, and we became friends. I don't know exactly when we decided that we would work as partners, it could have been my sixth beer, or his third Coca-Cola, but we were going to try our luck together.

Our hut in the mountains was better than most. True, it had no walls, but it did have a tin roof which kept us dry and stopped our floor from turning to mud during the long rainy season – the time when the young river running below our camp ate into its banks and threatened to carry us along – when the bush that surrounded us drank deeply and grew thick and strong and pushed nearer and nearer our hut, smothering the clearing we had worked so hard to cut, claiming back the land we had borrowed.

A long smooth wooden table stood in the centre of the hut. Benches made from logs carved with machetes ran down both sides. It was here we sat to eat the almost uneatable meals cooked by Antonio's wife Maria: sometimes half-cooked rice with boiled banana, or rice with fried banana, sometimes a little canned tuna while it lasted, always an avocado when in season – there was an avocado tree close to our camp. During one of these meals, Antonio first spoke to me about Juan Bravos. 'There is a bad man that lives near here, a dangerous man.' He began softly, as if Juan might suddenly enter our camp. 'He's not very tall, about your height, but much more powerful,' he continued, finally giving up on Maria's food and laying his spoon neatly next to his plate. 'He's an Indian, at least most of him is.

'He came from a drinking family, Indians are only trouble when they drink. When he was fourteen, he took a woman and started a family. Juan could do that because he could work, not like his father. He could also find gold, always found gold, the trouble was, he spent it just as quickly. Juan was never satisfied, he is never satisfied, he always wants more than God has promised.'

'God?' I queried.

'God!' he repeated through the haze made by his half-burned cigarette. 'Juan has no God, and if you have no God you live by no rules, you covet your neighbour's land, his house, his gold, his wife.'

'But I am not a Christian,' I pointed out, 'and I am an honest man, I am your partner.'

'You are a gringo,' he answered softly, tolerant of my ignorance. 'You do not need guidance, but we can be very bad men without it, very bad.'

Antonio sipped the sweet black coffee that Maria had made for us, and for a while said nothing. When he began again he spoke with an impassioned force I recognized from his lectures about his God. 'Bravos has murdered,' he screamed. Even Maria, who seemed to have little interest in anything, nodded her head slowly in support. 'In an area called Rio Oro, twenty miles to the north, that's why he's here, he had to leave.'

'How?' I asked even though I knew he would tell me anyway.

Antonio stood stretching his knotted muscles, Maria lit the candles although there was still light from the setting sun. 'Mining is a lonely life,' he started, 'months of eating bad food, working up to your waist in water twelve hours a day, breaking your back clearing rocks, and mostly finding nothing. A man can only take that for so long, then he looks for something to give him courage, or hope, or just to make him laugh. I found the Lord, but most just drink.' Antonio paced back and forth along the edge of our table, his fists clenched, his sharp small head nodding on his shoulders. He was angry, or frightened. Maria touched his shoulder as he passed. Howler monkeys moaned sadly from their high branches deep in the bush, bringing on the darkness. The first noises from the jungle night began.

'There's a tin shed in Rio Oro,' Antonio began again, 'just above the river line. It's the first settlement you come across heading back to the coast from the bush. It sells the supplies you need to keep mining. It also sells rum. It's a rougher country up there, steeper, more remote, rougher men too. Nicaraguan refugees, Cubans, the worst sort of criminals. The police never look for you in that country, never. Bravos was just one of many.

'Chancho Rodrigas was not one of the bad ones, but he could be trouble when he drank. He liked to fight. Bravos was passing on his way back to his gold diggings when Chancho, full of bottle courage, called him to fight with machetes. Bravos was leading a packhorse, the horse piled high with supplies. Juan answered only that he was a man, pulled out a .22 caliber rifle that nestled amongst the food on the horse's back and shot Chancho through the lungs.'

Antonio flicked his spent cigarette far into the blackness beyond our candlelight and stopped speaking. Suddenly, surprisingly, it had become much colder. The wind that moved through the bush around our hut became stronger.

'And now Juan Bravos is here.'

'Yes,' answered Antonio harshly, 'he is here. He wants my farm, he wants Maria, but I will kill him if he tries to take them.'

'But you are a Christian,' I reminded him.

'Yes,' he replied, 'I thought I was a good Christian, but when I think about Bravos I am not.'

The water sped past our thighs as we stood in the middle of the stream shovelling gravel into our sluice. We had just begun our work when they came. '*Manos arriba, manos arriba,*' a rough voice called to me, not loud, but urgent. I turned to face four men. The one who spoke was large, his face round and loose like a milk-fed baby's. His feet shuffled nervously, he was holding a gun. Antonio, knowing I still understood little Spanish, spoke quickly, 'He said, "Put your hands up".' I looked up towards the four men standing on the high bank beside the stream.

'Please,' begged Antonio, 'put your hands up.'

They left almost as quickly as they had come. They were not bandits but police, and they were not looking for us, they were looking for Juan Bravos.

We had been digging in the river most of the day when they returned. We had moved rock and dirt, our feet had been burned and blistered by the acid in the water, our hands were bleeding, and we had found almost nothing, but they had found Bravos. They marched him past, handcuffed and smiling. It was the first time I saw him and I was surprised at how young he was, how smooth and unlined his face was, save for a small scar just above his left eye. I looked to Antonio and felt his fear. Antonio, a small wiry man, was fifty-two, twenty-five years older than Juan. His wife Maria, squat, oval-faced and pretty, was only seventeen. If Bravos came for Maria, I understood completely that Antonio would have no chance.

The police held Juan for two weeks before they let him go. He had been charged with rape, but rape is hard to prove.

We left the mountains soon after Bravos had been taken away. We had been working for months and had found very little gold. I had been offered a job with an American mining company working the rivers far below: three meals a day, a bed and a wage. I was broke, I accepted. I brought Antonio and Maria with me. Now we would find gold for other people.

Over the next year, I would see Bravos passing our camp many times on his way down to the village on the coast to buy his supplies. Often he would sit and drink coffee with me. Sometimes we would sit alone, at times other men would join us, but they never stayed long. During these visits, I felt how afraid people were of him, and I saw how alone he was. A strange friendship grew between us, one which I could not explain to Antonio.

'He is a bad man,' Antonio would tell me after a visit, 'a bad man.' But when you sat with Bravos and listened, you knew that he was not all bad.

During these visits, Bravos would often leave his gun with us before continuing his trip into the village. He told me once he was afraid that when he drank he would shoot somebody. 'I just go a little crazy sometimes, I don't know why.' And I believed him. I had seen him fight twice in that year, both times with a madness that he could not control. I knew that had he been carrying his gun he would have used it.

*

During the year with the American miners I saw something I had not expected. I saw a gentle, charming, timid side of Juan Bravos. I saw Juan Bravos in love. Debbie was the daughter of the mine boss, an American. She had red hair and a round figure, not pretty, but full of life. I had heard her described as vibrant. She liked excitement and risk. She set her heart on Juan Bravos.

Bravos would walk the four hours to our camp almost every week, washing first in the river before he climbed the high bank where we had built our huts. Once there, he belonged to Debbie. At first I felt concern and fear for her, we all did, but in all that time Bravos was only gentle and courteous. She would drive him around like an emperor in the company jeep; he slept always in her tent, her passionate noisy tent. Her screams and moans mingled easily with the night sounds and became part of the jungle chorus that we listened to each evening. Juan only grunted.

Sometimes I would sit and drink whisky with them and she would make Juan take off his shirt and show me the hole a bullet wound had left in his shoulder. She loved being with a man somebody had tried to kill and couldn't.

When Debbie tired of him and chose another miner in our camp there was some trouble, but this was the trouble that always comes when a heart is broken and shamed. I felt pity for Juan Bravos, but I knew that his wife and children would be happy.

With our heavy machines we tore down jungle, diverted the river and dug up the earth the way a ravenous ill-mannered child eats his lunch. We dropped our gravel and earth into a long box, elevated and angled. We washed it through with water taken from the river and spewed from a huge hose. The gold lay trapped in our box and the earth became mounds of refuse at the other end. Small rocky hills of barren ugliness.

We were hungry; our company was not feeding us, at least not enough. Rice and beans, only rice and beans, meat was too expensive, at least that's what our American bosses thought. It takes a lot of money to mine gold in a Latin American jungle: diesel is expensive but necessary to run the earth-moving machines and the generators. Spare parts to mend broken parts were needed; they were imported. Whisky had to come from the capital, but our bosses would drink nothing else. Wages were cheap, we were paid little. Food was cheap and we were given only rice and beans. We were working for fools.

It was only a matter of time before trouble came. Our tractors would mysteriously break down, the men would refuse to work, water would be found in the diesel, the gold had to be watched very closely. We met beside the river to discuss the problems and find a solution. I spoke on behalf of the workers, and I was fired. The bosses paid the local police to guard the camp. The trouble finished.

Bravos had talked to me about going back into the mountains with him to work. I owned a water pump that would allow us to use the river water to wash a lot of dirt from the surrounding hills through our sluice. He could find the dirt that had trapped the gold. It should be a good partnership and I agreed, but I was afraid.

Antonio warned me against it. 'Stay here with us, with Maria and me,' he begged, 'I will talk to the bosses, they will take you back, God will not protect you with that man.' In the yellow light of the fire burning in darkness, his eyes danced as he spoke to me, the coffee that we drank was old and heavy.

When I explained that I couldn't stay he became restless, his hands played with his cup, spilling the liquid over his boots and onto the damp, dark earth. 'Why?' he asked.

'I will not work for these men again,' I answered. 'Bravos will find me gold.'

'Bravos will bring you trouble,' he said, rising and moving out of the light. '*Vaya con Dios.*'

*

Gold miners have to carry their own supplies into the mountains. They load rice, beans, canned tuna, bottled sauce, coffee, onions, garlic, sugar, oil, cigarettes, matches and always a little salt into an old hessian bag. They pack extra clothes, their gold pan, tie the top closed with a bit of old rope and then make a couple of pack straps. On top they tie their shovel, then they slip their arms through the straps and hoist it onto their backs. It can weigh fifty pounds. In their hands they carry a heavy iron bar to dislodge large rocks. If they're rich enough, they take a rifle to hunt.

To reach your mining camp you have to climb for five hours along trails that suck you down into mud that reaches your thighs. The trails are criss-crossed with roots and vines that unbalance you, trip you, slice at your cheeks as you stumble. There are vines that have to be cut with a machete before you can pass. The bush is so thick and the air so hot and wet that you have to suck in deeply to get any satisfaction. Your back bends more and more from the weight you're carrying, your hands are cut and bloody from your forward stumbles, and your legs become harder to pull free from their mud graves the further you go.

As well as the normal supplies we would have to pack, we were also going to be loaded down with a pump, hoses, and a fifteen-gallon container of gasoline. We would have to hire two extra men to help carry, but that would mean money, and that was in short supply. We brooded on this problem while sitting in a bar beside the dusty little road in the village on the coast. It was the same bar that I had met Antonio in, the only bar in town with a sea view. From our table you could look out over the inlet. It was very shallow and when the tide was low the water retreated, leaving a covering of deep black mud and mangrove. Large red crabs skated across the smooth surface dodging attacks from bare-footed mud-covered boys carrying long sticks, and from the starving dogs that roamed in hunting packs.

This was the place you landed when you came by boat from across the bay. The half-Chinese ferry captain always seeming to arrive at low tide, so that you were forced to slush through the mud over the crabs and around the dogs to shore. There was no jetty.

Holding his bottle of beer tightly with both hands, Juan took a small sip before suddenly throwing his head back and laughing loudly. 'I can get a horse, Wayne,' he said slowly, nodding his head. 'I can get a horse. Now we drink.'

The horse was white and old, tired and thin, it had sad eyes, bad breath, and it wasn't Juan's. 'It belongs to my brother-in-law, he's across the other side of the bay and will not be back until tomorrow's boat. I know where he keeps it. We pack our supplies up, and tomorrow I will bring the horse back down.'

We never returned the horse. Juan had never meant to. Every time I asked him about it, he simply replied that he would take it tomorrow. And now the brother-in law was at our camp to collect it. I thought at first that there would be no trouble, but the owner was a proud man and had been made to look a fool. Juan had taken his horse and had left him to wait on the coast like a begging man. When he first started to yell, Juan said nothing. Even Bravos knew the difference between right and wrong. But soon there was no question of right or wrong, Bravos was being insulted and he couldn't accept that. It had become a matter of honour. '*Hijo de puta*,' he screamed, as he pulled his machete free from its leather sheath. I know he would have killed the man, there was a madness in his look that told you that.

When Juan's brother-in-law first arrived, we were squatting around a smoking fire made from wet timber and green leaves, warming ourselves against the mountain jungle dampness, drinking coffee, talking. Besides Bravos and myself, there were three other miners who worked nearby. It took all four of us to wrestle the machete away from Bravos. If I had been alone, the horse owner would have died. During the scuffle one of the men slipped Juan's gun from its holster. Nobody trusted Bravos in a rage.

We worked for four months digging a deep narrow channel through the heart of a steep bank that stood guiding a newly-born stream. We dug to bedrock in a space barely wide enough to turn your shoulders, the banks on either side keeping us in the shadow most of the day. In the evenings we would cross the same river twice before we reached our hut made of poles and plastic. When rain stopped us from working, we would curl up and sleep like a cat after a meal, before a fire.

Once when we sat shivering, listening to driving rain dance on our plastic roof and watching the thick brown river rising and rising, I asked Bravos about the woman he had been accused of raping.

'I raped her,' he answered quickly, bowing his head before raising it again and smiling from the memory, 'and I would have raped Maria as well, in time.'

Every chance we had, we hunted. We came together with other miners, some had dogs, others rifles, everybody needed meat. We hunted wild pig, but also the tepezcuintle.

The dogs would scare this large rodent into the open and the chase was on. Over vines and through bush, down the hills and up again. At times the tepezcuintle was too quick for rifles to be of use, and then the dogs would run them down, ripping and tearing until we arrived to retrieve the kill. But not always. Some days the dogs were left panting far behind, their tongues dripping saliva, making mud in the earth, and if that happened, the tepezcuintle would find its hole because like rabbits, like gold miners, they were burrowers.

And then we would dig them out, or dig enough so that machetes could be driven through the earth into the unseen body. The only indication of a kill was the sensation of the machete passing through the hard stony soil and entering yielding, living flesh, and the muted, terrible squeals and cries that came from below the ground.

The meat of the tepezcuintle is fatty, but gold miners are lean, and the five pounds of flesh is quickly distributed.

At times we would see snakes on these hunting trips; sometimes we would see them when we walked to work, or when we returned to our hut after work, or in the morning when we took our first piss, but never at night when we took our last. The most dangerous snake was the Fer de Lance, but it was also the most common, though only a little more so than the small, lethal, bewitchingly striped coral snake that lurked along the river edge. Often we would see a green tree snake dangling elegantly, harmlessly from a branch, watching us curiously, impassively, or pass a python, fat and lazy, sunning itself beside the trail.

All of these snakes would slip fearfully into the safety of the underbrush if there was time, but if there was not, they would rear back, coil themselves and ready their head to strike. All the miners I knew were happy to allow the snake a retreat when it was possible to do so. Killing one always involved risk. Bravos did not care about the risk. I'm sure he didn't think about it. He would follow them into the longest grass laughing and squealing with excitement. 'A snake killed a friend of mine,' he explained one time, 'it took him twelve hours to die. We tried to carry him down the mountain but his pain was too much, he swelled, his skin darkened, we just laid him down and sat with him.'

Once I woke to find Bravos slashing the air with his machete.

Four vampire bats lay dead or dying on the ground, their bright red blood, maybe my blood, congealing into a dark angry blotch, wetting their fur. Another time I woke to the sound of gunfire, but it was only Juan shooting rats, he couldn't sleep. He had shot three.

We had been working for months and had found just enough gold to live from – it was time for me to leave. I had been working in Costa Rica for more than two years. I was tired of eating bad food, tired of the back-breaking work and the disappointment. Juan understood. 'I am an Indian,' he told me simply, placing his large work-scarred hand on my shoulder, 'I belong here.'

Juan moved his gear into the hut of another miner when I left. He explained that he was not afraid to sleep alone, he just liked the company. I knew better, I had seen him in the night too often.

The grey, slow-travelling clouds came almost to the rooftops, leaving no horizon. The air, heavy and wet, chilled you through your many layers of clothes. The light, no light. Narrow, stern, seventeenth-century houses looked haughtily down at the dull still waters of the canals. The trees lining the water were leafless, lifeless.

It had been eight months since I had left Costa Rica and moved to Holland. Amsterdam in December left you longing for the tropics, for the warm breezes, for the sun on your back. For the moment I had forgotten the hard work, the danger, the distress of trying to make a living on a gamble. The cold, dark, European winter makes you forget.

When the letter arrived I was surprised because it was my first from Costa Rica. It was from Antonio. Juan Bravos was dead, he wrote. There was no gloating in the letter, no relief, but also no sadness. Death by drowning was the official verdict. This *could* have happened of course: the rainy season had just ended in Costa

Rica and rain in the tropics was always to be respected. It was not so much the rain that was dangerous, but its accumulation and if it found a river to join forces with its strength would overwhelm anything in the way. Trees were uprooted and carried along like corpses on a sea of hands, great boulders would roll and slide in rhythm with the current, houses that had been built too close to the edge would slip into the river as elegantly as a boat being launched. To cross a river took a great deal of care. But I had crossed many with Juan, and he had crossed them all his life.

The police reported finding him trapped in the branches of a tree that had been uprooted and killed by the flood, and had simply buried him on the high bank next to the river. 'But nobody believed that,' wrote Antonio, 'Bravos was shot in the back of the head. That was common knowledge.'

Antonio finished his letter by telling me he had just had a baby with Maria, it was a boy, they had named him Miguel and all was fine. I placed the letter under a magazine that lay on a table near the window. In the grey Amsterdam afternoon light I wanted to forget it, but you can't so easily forget. Bravos was mostly bad. I kept thinking it didn't matter, but it did.

THE GOLD TRADE

The brown wooden saloon doors that you had to push through to enter The New York Bar had two functions: they let in light and air, bringing in the smells and life sounds of an arousing city that most couldn't stand parting with for very long. Their second function was privacy: people who wanted to look in had to peer over the doors like a child searching for food on a too high dinner table, or, if you were not tall enough, you could go down on your knees and look under and up, but in doing so you risked great humiliation if someone decided to leave. You could, of course, just open the swinging doors and go straight in as many people did, but for some that held risks: the bar could be empty and then you were more or less obliged to drink a beer alone. Or you could owe money to one of the drinkers sitting at the bar: many people owed money in 1983 in San José, Costa Rica. There could be a girl inside that you had no wish to see because, the night before, your fantasies had exceeded your libido – or her moral borders. Or perhaps the girls had not arrived yet, and there is nothing lonelier than sitting in a whore bar, which the New York was, without whores.

At the time, I was earning my living buying gold on the Peninsula de Osa in the south of Costa Rica near the border with Panama, and selling it in the capital, San José. I thought The New York Bar would be a good place to sell – if there were drinkers inside.

Business had not been bad lately, my gold was moving. Tonight I would just put my shoulders back, push straight through those doors, and if I had to wait, then I would do so drinking cold beers with a patient heart.

It was still early and the customers, all of whom sat on tall bar stools around the straight, glass-topped bar, stared absently into their drinks, or looked expectantly into the mirror behind the bar; some to catch their own reflections, but most, who had no need to be reminded that they were not as young as they used to be, to watch for the girls coming in to work that night, who also peered over or under the door checking for customers.

The mirror was gold framed, and so large that you could see most of the bar in reflection: the photo of the New York skyline hung on the far wall above the jukebox that played hip-moving Latin rhythms or soul-searching cowboy ballads; the dark mahogany booths with maroon, plastic-covered seats that were more comfortable when you were sitting with a girl; the swinging doors that meant so much to the course of the evening. A large stuffed fish hung directly above the mirror, photos of men holding smaller fish hung beside it.

A cold bottle of Imperial beer stood waiting for me on the bar as I mounted a stool. As I groped for my wallet, Steve, the bar manager, whispered that it was on the house. Maria, a beaming, frizzy-haired Creole, stood beside him waiting to serve the gringos – because only gringos could afford the price of the drinks and the girls.

'When did you get back?' asked a thin, deeply-lined man sitting two stools down.

'Three days ago, Jim, pull your stool over. Give Jim a drink, Maria.' Maria, who was not a working girl, would always rub her hand along mine when she gave me my change. She liked to flirt with me, with everybody, but I liked it when it was me.

The bar started to fill. The cigarette smoke became thick and the noise so thunderous that the jukebox became useless. Baseball-capped men, Americans mostly, stood drinking away the cool San José night with each other. The girls, who were all shades of brown and all degrees of beautiful, but by no means all young or slim, had also flocked in. They stood around chatting, preening themselves, trying to catch the eye of one of the Americans, but they never pushed themselves on to men who were not ready or not interested. It was a rule in The New York that if men wanted to drink they were to be left alone, and the men must treat the girls with courtesy and respect. Many long friendships had developed between the girls who needed the extra money and the men who needed once in a while to be loved and had the twenty dollars to pay.

'You're back, ya little bastard!' I turned to see Robert towering over me. He held his beer in his fleshy hand as if ready to club me with it. Robert was an ex-boxer whose pugilistic heart still beat strong. This at times made him a lively drinking partner if not always a relaxed one. From our many conversations I learned that he was a light heavy who had boxed in England in the sixties. Robert was good, but I only had his word to go by. His smashed, boneless nose and slowed speech indicated that his defence was not all it should have been. I only ever saw Robert in the New York and we only ever talked about boxing, so I was surprised when he asked me how the gold mining was going. 'Finished with the mining, Robert,' I replied. 'I sold my equipment, the pump, the hoses, the lot. I'm just trying to get enough cash together to get the hell out of here.'

'You wanta get outta fucking paradise?' He screamed to make his point, wiping the back of his hand across his nose and sniffling as he often did after a sentence.

'Listen Robert, when you're arse-deep in muddy water shovelling tons of dirt through a sluice box trying to catch a bit of gold, it don't seem like paradise. And then there's the bad food, rice and beans, beans and bloody rice, not to mention the rain and cold, the leaking huts that you have to live in, the rats and vampire bats that play with any bits of your body that are left uncovered at night, no beer for weeks on end, only the company of unwashed men and the snakes.'

'Snakes,' he spat back. Snakes, I knew, were the only thing Robert's bruised brain would let him be afraid of, the only thing that really impressed him.

'Yeah,' I continued, 'had to kill one the last trip, must have been three metres long, a bushmaster, split him in two with my machete, one slice.'

'Un-fucking-believable,' was all I heard as Robert left, heading towards the men's, 'un-fucking-believable.'

'Is that true, Macca?' asked Steve, who had been cleaning glasses and listening to the conversation.

I touched Steve's arm and smiled before I answered, 'No, mate, it was a bushmaster but it was only about two metres long, and I didn't kill it. Like a bloody fool I was running back out of the mountain. You never run in the mountains, too many things to stand on, but I was feeling good, heading down for a cold beer. I'd just spent a couple nights buying gold from a few miners I'd worked with.'

'That's what you're doing now then, is it?' asked Steve, leaning closer to hear over the noise that was building.

'Yeah, without equipment you can't mine, so I buy nuggets from my old mates at good prices. They make great earrings, rings, they look good hanging on chains. Anyway, I put a thirty per cent mark-up on the nuggets and sell them to your countrymen.'

'Nice business!' said Steve, winking. 'Now finish the snake story before Joe Palooka gets back from throwing punches at the mirror in the toilet.'

A group of men pushed through the swinging doors, casting out greetings to other drinkers as if they had suddenly found back their lost tribe. They were regulars, men who kept The New York Bar till ringing and the girls eating. Steve moved quickly to serve them. I waited, enjoying my beer until he returned, and then continued.

'As I said mate, I was running through mud. Heavy deep stuff. The trail had been churned up by rain the night before, and there was a thick pearl-coloured mist mixed into the bush. I couldn't see too far, but I didn't mind it because it was wet, and it left me feeling damp and clean all over. I'd just reached the top of a rise on the trail before it dropped down to a creek bed, when this bushmaster reared up in front of me. Mate, I stopped as if I'd just hit a wall. His head was arched over his body, and his eyes just stared at me.'

'And,' asked Steve, leaning closer.

'Well, I can't really say I did anything consciously, but I reached for my machete and at the same time started moving backwards. I suppose my brain had decided that was the smartest thing to do. At the time we were about a metre apart. I got my knife about halfway out before my foot caught a root that had wormed across the trail, and I fell arse over head. The bushmaster started to back away from me, still in a striking position, but moving backwards, and as I struggled to right myself from the mud, he just wheeled around, fell flat, and slithered into the bush.

'It's thick rainforest up there, I suppose he was using the trail to sun himself. After it had finished, I slipped down to the creek bed and sat for a long time on a rock in the middle of the stream dousing my head with the cold water. Mate, the snake had scared the hell out of me.' Steve smiled, shook his head and turned to serve another customer.

'Did you do any buying at Dos Brazos?' asked Jim, who had been half-listening, half-romancing a plump black girl who had sat down next to him. Everybody knew Jim was involved in selling shares in a gold mine at Dos Brazos on the Rio Tigre. The New York was Jim's office. Steve brushed his long thin hair back out of his eyes, wiped his beer-wet hands and leaned over the bar towards Jim, 'Why the fuck don't you know what's going on in your own goddamn mine, Jim?'

'It ain't my mine, and you ain't getting me down there amongst the snakes and mad fuckers.'

'Jim,' I interrupted, 'your mine is doing fine. They're working pockets. They turn the river this way and that way, then they take their front-end loaders and begin ripping the ground up at likely spots and run it through their sluice boxes. Now, some people would say that you're going to miss a lot of gold that way, others would say that if you're in a hurry to get in and out quickly with the most profit, that's the method to use. They leave their tailings piled up and scattered around like abandoned anthills, and the land they've worked through is cratered and dead. If you look down at it from the jungle in the hills, it looks like an infected wound, all pus and scab, and the river that runs below is thickly silted, brown; that's the wound weeping.

'But you know, Jim, that one square mile piece of eaten earth is feeding hundreds of people. They're digging in the tailings and finding plenty of missed gold. There are three *pulperias* open to feed and supply the miners, there's a bar that I wouldn't advise drinking in alone, there are trucks hauling supplies and diesel, there's even a telephone service out there, hand operated. So Jim, that's how it is, but I got to warn you, when I flew up here, some of your boys from the mine, the fat one that waddles and the Tico with the family in government, were loading something small that took four men to lift into a single-engined plane, and you know how heavy gold is. Anyway, that plane flew straight to Panama and we both know that all gold has to be sold to the Costa Rican Government.'

'The sons of bitches,' yelled Jim, not getting any attention in a bar full of men who were all yelling to be heard.

'Yeah, I'd say that's what they were,' put in Steve smiling, 'but since you don't actually own any shares, I'd say the big losers were the poor silly bastards you're selling to, and if you stopped selling, then nobody would lose.'

'And how the fuck am I supposed to eat and drink?' replied Jim, agitated, drawing deeply on his cigarette.

'Take it easy, Jim,' I whispered, 'they're probably recording it in their bookkeeping, your clients are going to make a packet.'

Jim turned and again started to romance the plump Negrita wearing too-tight white jeans and a red shiny synthetic tank top that held up breasts that had fed many children. He had heard enough about gold mines for one night.

I started thinking about bringing my gold out when Steve stopped me.

'Wait a bit, Macca, there are a few strangers here tonight, Costa Ricans, you know it's illegal for gringos to be dealing in gold. Let's wait and see what happens, I don't want any trouble. Besides, I think the boss might want to have a look, I know he likes the stuff, and he always wants first choice.'

'I've got time, mate,' I answered, taking another long sip, enjoying the crowd, watching the girls.

The owner of The New York Bar was late coming that night, but when he did arrive the Costa Ricans who were strangers hadn't left. 'Come into the back, Macca,' he suggested, 'I want to see those nuggets. Got any with a bit of quartz in them?'

All the nuggets I had with me came from the Rio Tigre, a river that began as a humble stream high in the jungle mountains, matured swiftly and fell, winding, twisting and gouging downwards through the rainforest towards the sea. The gold that the Tigre carried churned, bounced upwards and outwards, jammed behind rocks, settled at the bottom of waterfalls, became discarded in the eddies as the river wound along the contours of the mountains looking for the quickest way down. It was only near the sea that the Tigre became wide and gentle enough to have the time and motion to grind the lumps of gold into dust, gold dust. I bought all my gold on the upper reaches where there was no shortage of good nuggets.

Tigre gold had a red hue, a copper light, and a lot of it was still bound with the quartz that had mothered it deep in the heart of earth. The river polished and shaped it. I had half moons, only a little distorted from their grinding trip, gold that looked like hearts, I had thick chunky nuggets and fine smooth ones, I even had one that looked like Australia. Some of my gold pieces were blazoned with quartz, others were riddled with it, reminding some of a skin pigment disorder.

'That's the one I want, that big mother with the flecked quartz.'

I had one more beer, a talk with Robert about heavyweight fighters, and then said my goodbyes. I thought I would try another bar before I got too drunk.

I pushed through the swinging doors onto the night street that still moved at the pace of young feet dancing to a salsa beat. Traffic rolled past, people strolled by. Everybody looking for action or hunting for girls who stood on the street corners waiting for them.

'*Tiene fuego?*' he called from the middle of the road, coming towards me, watching for traffic, coming closer.

'No, *amigo*,' I don't have a light, I answered back, turning to face him. He was young and tall and excited, and I knew he didn't need a light. Another two young men came from a little further up, moving to stand beside him like horses competing in a carousel.

'*Que tiene alla?*' '*Que tiene?*' one yelled, making the nerves in his neck twitch. His feet shuffled.

'Nada,' I have nothing, I screamed back just as loudly, moving back up against the wall and taking a step back towards the swinging doors.

'*Quien son ustedes?*' '*Policia, que tienes alla?*' 'Bullshit, *mierda*,' I answered, moving again towards the swinging doors but coming up against another two men who had come out of the darkness that lurks between street lamps. Now there were five.

'*Que tiene?*' '*Que tiene?*' asked the first, who was still dancing from foot to foot. '*Somos policia*,' he screamed again but now his voice was less sure. He looked to his friends. I waited for them to come but instead they kept moving nervously, directionless, without a plan.

The girls drifted by unconcerned. Horns of passing cars howled at the night. I held tightly onto my gold, to all that I owned.

'*Somos policia, que tiene alla?*' It was the two men from the bar, they were older, paunchier, calmer. They wore ties and jackets and confidence.

'How do I know you're police?' I asked, knowing that they were. One of the men pulled back his jacket, letting me glimpse his pistol. Convincing me that such questions were irrelevant.

'*Tengo oro, solamente oro*,' all I got is gold, sir, only gold. The boys, who were not nervous any more, took turns holding the plastic bag full of nuggets. '*Que linda, linda*,' how beautiful, beautiful, was all they could say as they felt the gold that shone dull under the street lights. I could only watch like a fox that had been fenced out of the chicken yard, hoping that the nuggets didn't disappear.

'You have no drugs?' asked the second suited man in perfect English.

'No,' I answered quickly, 'no drugs, just gold.'

'From the Osa?' they asked.

'Yeah, the Osa.'

'A lot of snakes on the Osa.'

'Crawling with them,' I answered.

'Good luck then, we were looking for drugs, we heard drugs were being sold in the gringo bars. Cocaine, we thought you were selling cocaine.'

'*Buenos noches.*'

'*Buenos noches,*' I answered, six more *buenos noches* came back at me.

After they had gone, I stood fingering my gold, following the smooth lines, sanding my fingers on the rough quartz, feeling my wealth. A girl gently rubbed against me in passing, she gazed back over her shoulder, smiled and stopped, waiting for an answer. I shook my head slowly from side to side, turned back to The New York Bar and pushed through the swinging doors.

PAT'S GOLD

My need to return was unexpected, powerful. Fourteen years after leaving Costa Rica I decided to go back. Forgetting that you can't go back. It was only later I understood that many men have this need to return. All of them forgetting, as I did, that it's impossible.

To start looking for gold again in Central America after so many years was not going to be easy. It was never safe working alone and for a stranger it held a greater risk. I had to have a partner, someone who was known and respected.

From my old friend Antonio's last letter, written many years before, I understood that he had found a good job in town and that Maria had run off with another miner, taking their son Miguel with her. Antonio had mentioned that Patrick O'Connell was still working in gold. I couldn't think of a better man to work with. I decided to look for Pat.

When we met again after all those years I found him twenty pounds heavier but otherwise unchanged. He wore the same large smile as if the world were a circus and he had a front row seat. He still moved like a cat stepping between broken glass and, as in my memory, his light-blue eyes twinkled only with delight, never malice. I explained why I had come. Pat smiled and told me he had been waiting for me.

'It was just a feeling, a very strong feeling,' he explained to me, 'I don't know how it came myself.'

For a moment he said nothing and then suddenly shouted, 'We're going to Nicaragua to buy gold.' Sweat dribbled across his round red face, his curly ginger hair stood to attention in the wet heat. 'Mano has been telling me about it for years, San Carlos, on the Rio Coco, that's where the gold is.'

'Who's Mano?' I asked, staring hard at him, wondering if he was serious.

'Mano is a Miskito Indian, he's been working around here since the war in Nicaragua.'

'Is he coming with us?' I asked, perplexed.

'No, Mano's always drunk. He was a good miner but he'll never go back. Not now.'

Pat sat heavily on a broken stool that stood next to his small green Formica-topped eating table as if the weight of all the good men who were now drunks had suddenly been placed on his shoulders, and stared through the open door over a stand of blood-red hibiscus towards the gentle blue bay. It seemed minutes until he began to speak again.

'I've been waiting for a partner, somebody honest, who's not a drunk. One who knows what he's doing. And now you're here.'

'What about mining in Costa Rica, on the Osa?' I asked.

'You look in the mirror lately? You're fourteen years older.' Pat stopped talking again and swallowed from a bottle of rum, handed the clear strong liquid to me and began again. 'I reckon you could still manage the back-breaking work in the mountains, you still look strong enough, but do you remember what it was like: always being wet and dirty, eating rice and beans three times a day, dodging snakes and thieves, never being able to drink a cold beer for weeks on end? Why would you want to do that? And besides, we'll make a lot more money buying and selling. Nicaragua, that's the place. Oh there's a lot of gold, a lot more than Costa Rica ever had, and it's remote. Hell, here it's just got too civilized. It makes you old.'

When I first met Pat he was living with his Costa Rican wife and four small children in a remote stretch of mountainous jungle on the northern edge of the Osa Peninsula. He had built a house on a high bank overlooking a muddy narrow creek from rough-milled timber that had been hauled up from the coast by horseback. Next to the house stood a small tin shed. From inside the shed, which was unshaded and furnace-hot, he sold shovels, bars, pans, flour, rice, sugar, matches, candles and rum. The shop was also the local bar. Sometimes there were fistfights. At other times customers fought with machetes. Two men were shot in front of Pat's shop, one died.

Sometimes Pat's wife would take care of the business and Pat would pan a little gold, or do what he did best: buy and sell it. All of his buying was done after dark. Pat would go out under black-wet skies, or on nights so clear from a full round moon that a flashlight was not necessary. It was all the same to him. Often he would walk thirty kilometres over muddy, vine-scarred, snake infested trails searching out the mining camps that were scattered through the bush like the lean-to's of nomads. He would sleep beside the trail, pissing in his pants to save time, eating only pan-fried bread.

When I asked him about his habits years before, he told me, surprised at my interest, that he was wet from crossing the rivers anyway, and that he travelled at night because thieves have to sleep sometime. And if you knew Pat, you knew that there were some things he never joked about.

But that was then: Pat had long since left his shop in the bush and gone off with another woman, who had since gone off with another man. His children had been sent to live with Pat's brother in the United States and Pat had gone to live in the banana port of Golfito.

Golfito is built on the edge of a bay within a bay. It stands pressed against the water by a jungle-smothered mountain ridge that rises steeply up behind it. Expansion in any direction other than further along the water's edge is impossible. It is a pencil-thin line of civilization at the mercy of sea and jungle.

Golfito is colourful, scruffy, and full of small, mean bars. Bars that are constantly crowded with drunks who drink in rhythm with the salsa music which plays loudly and constantly. The heat is wilting, but the women, who have been whoring for three generations, are friendly and plentiful.

If you look down on Golfito from a high point, far enough away not to smell the tidal garbage, from a distance great enough to filter the noise and distort the imperfections, you could mistake it for paradise.

We planned to leave for the north just as soon as an old gold-mining friend of Pat's got back from hospital. The miner, whose name was Bonanzio, had been staying with Pat when his heart started pounding hard in his chest and his breathing became a wheeze. Sadly he never did get back: he died of a heart attack, alone on an early morning following a sweltering night.

'He was like a father to me,' Pat told me in a sad even voice. 'I have to organize the funeral.' After notifying the family, who lived many miles away in the capital, he chose a coffin. He bought one made from spruce with a grey-fur-lined lid, because he knew Bonanzio would have liked the fur.

Bonanzio needed to be made ready for the last viewing: he had to look his best. He was collected from the hospital and whisked off to the undertaker who pumped him full of a soft-pink solution. But it is savagely hot in Golfito, things rot quickly, ice was needed, too. This Pat purchased from a small fish factory at the end of the bay, carrying it back in dripping hessian sacks.

Pat used his own house for the last viewing. People crowded in, crying, drinking and crying. Shrouded in his cloak of ice, Bonanzio smiled thirstily. Time was running out, the ice started melting. He was taken quickly to the cemetery. The rest should have been dignified and easy but the gravediggers had not dug the hole wide enough. Bonanzio's coffin stuck as it was being lowered. Three of the largest mourners had to stand on the box while other men levered it with shovels, forcing it to the bottom.

The women began to howl and scream when they realized that Pat had not taken the ice out. 'He hates water,' wailed a middle-aged daughter. Images of Bonanzio floating unhappily in his fur-lined coffin filled my thoughts. That night we all drank to his honour, and left early, shakily, the next day for Capital.

The bus ride to San José hadn't changed in fourteen years. Eight hours of swinging and swaying on a winding road over a wild, cloud-covered mountain range called Cerro De La Muerte (Death Hill). In the fourteen years since I had ridden the bus, I had forgotten the recklessness of the Costa Rican bus drivers, the bravado that gives them the power to turn the bravest man into a coward, make the strongest stomach weak, convert a faithless man. Pat dozed, woke and dozed again, always at peace.

Halfway down the northern side of the Cerro De La Muerte, our bus arrived at an old Spanish town called Cartago. It was night and as usual it was very dark. I turned in my seat to give myself a better view and gazed downwards across a wide valley floor and saw a mosaic of lights, sparkling, beckoning. They were the lights of San José.

In the old days nothing thrilled me more than this sight. It meant good food, a real bed, women, and it meant the Nashville South.

The Nashville South was a downtown bar. It had swinging doors onto the street. Its interior was roughly finished wood and the bar, which was not long, was highly polished. Flags from different states of the Union hung from the ceiling. A large picture of Willy Nelson decorated the back wall. When you drank in the Nashville South you listened to cowboy music.

It was my bar, a place I came to when I wanted to feel at home although I was a long way from home. Jack, the gringo owner, became a close mate, and the other drinkers, family. But Pat had already explained to me that Jack was dead.

'Cancer – Jack just couldn't give the smokes up.' Pat also made it clear that the new owner was a cranky old bastard and that the new customers were not the same type of men as before.

'How do you mean?' I asked.

'Tourists, that's all they are, tourists.' I made up my mind to leave the past where it belonged. We would find a new place to drink. We chose a sports bar called Tiny's. There were four television sets, each one secured high, close to the ceiling, and facing a different part of the bar. Gum-chewing men in striped uniforms and small peaked caps played baseball on two of the sets. On the other two, tall muscular black men, athletic and elegant, were throwing a round ball into a hoop. At times a white man appeared, less muscular, more plodding. We were both drinking rum with Coca-Cola, ice but no lemon. We picked slowly at the nuts on the bar.

We were on our second drink when Pat reached awkwardly into his pants pocket, fiddled for a moment, and then pulled out a small eight-armed figurine that he laid carefully on the bar.

'A god,' he said when he saw me looking. From the other pocket came a frog with a small bell attached to its neck. 'I got to sell some gold,' he finally explained to me, 'they're pre-Columbian, I've had them for years. It's my share in Nicaragua.' Pat leaned towards the bartender who was hovering, waiting for an order. 'Where can I get rid of these?' he asked, pushing the figurines towards the man. The Costa Rican bartender nodded in the direction of a thin, nervous-looking man at the end of the bar.

His name was Corporal Love. 'The best sport fishing captain in Costa Rica,' he told us by way of introduction, 'and the best marine sniper in Vietnam, over three hundred kills.' Pat, who had served in Korea and had little time for people with war stories, sneered a little before he pushed the gold towards the captain who said, 'I know a man who'll be interested. You'll make good money, less my commission of course.' He then turned towards the toilets, 'Got to piss,' he called back to us. Immediately a small old gringo shuffled in beside us at the bar, 'Don't trust that son of a bitch, he'll rob you before you turn around,' he whispered before disappearing into the group of cheering men watching the tall black athletes throwing the round ball.

A short taxi ride later, Pat, myself and Corporal Love stood before a square, two-storey, light-blue building. Each floor had three tall, round-topped windows. Heavy maroon curtains kept out the light, thick iron grates barred intruders. The man who opened the door was massive and roughly bearded. He wore a black Hell's Angel T-shirt and jeans held up with braces. He led us through a hall with rooms either side filled with massage tables. Girls wearing short synthetic skirts and tiny tank tops, or wrapped in worn, white towels wandered past. A sauna spewed out heat at the end of the corridor. Pat turned to me, 'The guy's a fucking pimp!'

I smiled, thinking about how much time Pat had needed to work that out, before I answered, 'What the fuck do you care? You're always fucking whores.'

'In Golfito they work alone. I hate fucking pimps.'

167

A door beside the sauna led us out to a patio where chairs and a table had been set up. Pat placed the figurines on the table and we waited. Our buyer's voice boomed as he shouted questions at us: 'Is this stuff real? Did you find them? Where did they come from?' He then explained to us carefully and slowly, that he would kick our arses if it was not real.

As Pat's hands moved quickly towards the figurines, anger painting his face a crimson red, Corporal Love moved his chair back. I waited for the explosion, but it never came. The buyer realized he had made a mistake, his palms faced skywards as he mumbled an apology. He bought both pieces. We closed the deal with a whisky and paid Corporal Love his commission in the taxi driving back to the bar.

As we entered Tiny's, the televisions blared their welcome, and the small old gringo who had warned us about the captain waved at us. I smiled and nodded at him, he grinned back, happy at our luck.

The next morning we were off to Nicaragua. Another bus trip, a small dispute with immigration, and there we were, Managua, the capital of Nicaragua.

The civil war that had bloodied Nicaragua for a decade was over. The Sandinistas had been defeated in a democratic election and Violetta Chamorro was the new president. There were still armed groups roaming the hills not satisfied with peace, but there are always people not satisfied with peace. Bandits had become a problem along lonely stretches of road in faraway provinces, but there had always been bandits.

Pat hadn't slept for two days. San José doesn't let you rest. As soon as we arrived in Managua he fell into a sleep that would last fifteen hours. I found a bar that served ice-cold beer for drinking and warm chicken with beans for eating. One that exclusively, continuously, played 'Los Broncos', a Latin cowboy sound that warmed your heart and boiled your blood, and I found mates to drink with, so long as I was buying – and I was.

Managua is not a place you care to linger. It was destroyed during the earthquake of 1972, leaving in its place a graveyard of steel, collapsed concrete and hovels. The old dictator, Anastasio Somoza, stole the money donated to rebuild it and the Sandinistas who replaced him never seemed to do any better.

We stayed just a single day, our destination was Waspan, the capital of Misquitia on the Rio Coco, the border with Honduras. Travelling overland was going to take us a week, so our plan was to fly to Puerto Cabezas in the north, and from there catch a truck for the eight-hour ride to Waspan.

During the civil war the Sandinistas had been supported and financed by the Soviet Union. This meant that anything that was motor-powered was Soviet built. As we climbed aboard a Lot, the Soviet-built twin-engined plane that flew us to Puerto Cabezas, I heard Pat whispering to himself, 'Commie shit, Commie shit.' Pat was a Republican. The oath was repeated, when we found our seats ripped and the belts broken, and then repeated again. Pat was even less happy when he saw the great hulking overcrowded truck that would carry us on the last part of our journey to Waspan. 'Another Russian piece of garbage,' was all he would say.

The road to Waspan winds its way through a forest of pine. It is a vast, empty savannah that begins near the coast and reaches far inland. Indian villages are scattered untidily beside the road and others are built deep into the forest leaving the Miskitos long walks to reach their only connection to another world. The road is bumpy and full of holes but it is all they have and nobody seems to complain.

Since the war there had been problems with armed groups attacking and robbing trucks travelling these roads. The bandits preferred the rainy season, because the bad roads caused by the heavy rain slowed the progress of the trucks. It was now the rainy season. A policeman armed with a regulation AK47 rode guard on our truck, but I didn't reckon on one copper doing much, and Pat had even less confidence. We were relieved to arrive with the ten thousand dollars we had left Costa Rica with.

Waspan's main street runs perpendicular to the river. Before the war it had been a thriving town where produce was brought from other points along the Rio Coco to be sold and transported to all parts of Nicaragua and further afield. Chinese traders and the Miskito Indians had made it into the most important rural headquarters in the region. During the war, the Sandinistas destroyed Waspan and relocated the people. Now four years into the peace, it had risen from its own cold ashes. It had not grown back to its previous glory, or size, but its two discotheques, playing mostly Miskito music, and uncountable bars made it a cacophony of sound that could easily fool you into believing it was much larger.

It took us two days to find a boat going upriver. Days that we filled with beer drinking in the breeze beside the water, and long drunken afternoon sleeps in a tiny, sweltering hotel room the heat of which left us hung-over and drenched in sweat.

The Rio Coco is a long meandering watercourse, easily navigable for most of the year, presenting problems only during heavy rains when it becomes wide and bullying. The villages along its path had been built as clusters of wooden houses on high banks far back from the edge. The elevated houses consisted of two parts: a large cooking hut connected by a wooden pathway to a sleeping hut. Grand wooden churches dominated every village skyline. Their spires stabbing the sky, dwarfing the surroundings. Papaya and banana trees gave shade. Vegetables grew in small well-guarded plots. Pigs roamed.

At each village we passed, half-naked women stood waist deep in water, washing, beating their clothes against a flat rock where the river idles by the bank; together, happy. Pat stared, intrigued and charmed. 'I've never seen women who enjoy washing so much, the clothes must be as clean as hell,' he observed to no one in particular.

'Yeah, they're clean,' replied one of our fellow passengers who had been listening. And then, laughing fiercely through broken teeth, 'they just wear out quickly.'

I had been told that you could make it upriver in a day, but if your boat was slow and overcrowded it would take one and a half days. Ours was very slow and dangerously overcrowded. People and goods were packed in tightly, intimately. Hands accidentally touched bare legs, caressed thighs. Water lapped at the gunnels.

We reached the village of Santa Fé after dark. This was to be our night stop. As luck would have it, Santa Fé and two neighbouring villages were combining their resources and holding a celebration. Sadly it was of the religious kind, and there wasn't a real drink in sight. This party, I now realized, was the reason I had seen so many canoes being paddled so frantically upriver.

'And all to sing church hymns and eat fried pig meat washed down with black thick coffee,' observed Pat a little sadly.

That evening, along with our twelve co-passengers, we were given space to sleep on the floor of a hut. It's tradition that a village provides lodging when night stops your boat. You never pay. Pigs and chickens had been killed, and the black thick coffee was always boiling. We feasted soberly.

In the morning we were off again. Faced with the prospect of only a half day of travelling ahead of us, Pat was agitated, restless, like an addicted smoker who has just dropped his last packet in the river. I understood how he felt. Most of the other passengers still had some more travelling to do. They lived past San Carlos, above the rapids, and would have to change boats later that day. (Ours could not make it: it was too big.) They made their living through gold mining and farming. They all looked poor, but strong. During the trip, their leader, a man called Adolfo, older and leaner than the others, told stories, sang songs and pantomimed continuously. And when he thought one of his efforts particularly funny, he would translate it into Spanish for us. We learned from Adolfo that in his view Miskito women had a particularly exciting sex life, because Miskito men were the best lovers in the world.

Adolfo had spent the last two months in Waspan, where his daughter had been treated for a leg infection. These infections I knew could kill very quickly in the tropics if left unattended. And now he was travelling back with a healthy daughter, and no money, at least until he borrowed some from me and Pat.

Still he had earned it; whenever our motor man would try to overload us with too much cargo, Adolfo was always the first to complain. On behalf of everyone. He had become our leader as well.

We arrived in San Carlos on the afternoon of the second day. This was where we would find our gold, everybody said so. San Carlos was richer than the other villages along the river. Its houses were bigger, most were painted, there were more cows, pigs. It was here that an old and famous gold mine existed. If you could smell gold, San Carlos would stink.

We found a place to sleep and then went in search of gold to buy. And we found it, the beautiful fine, clean, twenty-two carat stuff. This was Pat's greatest love, gold in its purest natural form. Gold that had risen from deep in the earth and had travelled, always going wherever the river chose to take it, until it was allowed to rest where the water gentled. Often it had become so worn and fine that only dust was left. Gold dust.

But we couldn't buy any of it.

Hondurans, the neighbours to the north, had recently started buying gold for a much higher price than we could afford to pay. They were reselling to the war-savaged country of El Salvador where gold it seemed was the only currency they could trust. The Hondurans were buying everything coming out of the mine, there was nothing left for us. We had travelled a long way for nothing.

I made arrangements to take a boat back the next day. Pat was downcast and beaten. We had to find a bar and quick. We did, San Carlos has only one.

Along the river there are many tributaries and in almost all you find gold. What ends up in San Carlos is remarkably pure but in many of the creeks miners dig for gold that has been corrupted by other metals. Gold that has mated with silver, or perhaps copper. Usually it lies in a bed of heavy black sand and to retrieve it you have to use mercury. After burning off the mercury (a dangerous process for man and nature if not done right) you are left with an impure, low-quality gold. Usually it is an ugly lump of metal that bears no resemblance to gold. In the absence of chemicals to test its true content, its value is determined solely by colour. It was this gold that an Indian miner offered to sell to us.

He sat nursing a cheap rum, when we arrived. We discovered that he was also trying to drown his sorrows. Nobody wanted to buy his gold. The Hondurans didn't want it, they wanted the pure stuff. Hell, we would buy it.

His mood was not good, but then neither was Pat's. It wasn't the best atmosphere in which to conduct a business deal. This proved true a few minutes later when I turned to speak to the miner and saw that he was moving backwards, hands held high, blocking as best he could the lefts and rights being thrown at him by my little mate.

By the time the fight had started both of them were pretty drunk, so they were not too difficult to separate. But we still had to buy the gold. How to begin again? First new rums were bought and the blood wiped away. Hands were shaken, civility more or less restored. Not easy when the problem is between two drunks who have no common language or reason to be friendly.

But in the end we wanted to buy and he wanted to sell. There was still plenty of spitting and shouting, but a deal was made. We had finally bought some gold.

We had covered our costs with our purchase but it was no business. Pat took the little single-engined bush plane back to Managua the day after we arrived in Waspan. He would sell the gold and forward my money. I took a truck out the same day to the coast. I had decided to stick around Nicaragua, Costa Rica had changed too much, or I hadn't changed enough.

GONE FISHING

Puerto Cabezas is built facing inland as though it is too terrified to look towards the unpredictable and often wild sea. It has no bay. History forced it into becoming a seaport. Wealth had to be shipped out, and Puerto Cabezas was chosen. It does have a slight windbreak caused by a barren point of land that juts eastwards, forcing the wind from the north around the long jetty which was built by the Standard Fruit Company eighty years before to load their bananas, and later made possible the export of gold from the mines in the hinterland. The jetty now gives refuge to the rusting shrimp fleet; to the lobster diving boats, their decks littered with air tanks and paddle canoes; to Indian sail dories that prowl the coast hunting turtle, and at times to the small cargo ships that trade the Caribbean.

These days, the jetty creaks and sways, as the surf rolls against it. Its piles are rotting and the holes left by missing planks make walking along it an exercise best left to the agile. But it is still the pumping heart of Puerto Cabezas.

I had arrived in this northern Nicaraguan town just a week before, from the Rio Coco, the long meandering watercourse that marks the border between Nicaragua and Honduras. I had been buying gold in the hope of reselling it at a profit in Costa Rica, the neighbour to the south. The trouble was, I was paying more for the gold than I could sell it for. The gold buyers from Honduras had pushed the price sky-high and my clients, the jewellery shops in Costa Rica, would only pay rock-bottom prices. I needed to earn a living, it had become time to look for another business. But what?

Ever since I was old enough to think about my life, I reasoned that it would be nice to be rich or to do something important, but I knew that wasn't likely to happen. What I could control, however, were two things: How I would live and where. I decided I would never stay doing one job all my life, and that I was going to live away from my home town, far away. I had since worked in many places doing many things. I had been a bank clerk, a slaughterhouse worker, I had boxed professionally, I had worked as a construction worker, a deckhand on a salmon fishing boat in Alaska, as a gold miner in Costa Rica, a silk buyer in China, a dishwasher, a tree planter, a barman, a waiter. There had been other jobs.

All along the jetty men shouted and howled, boats were unloaded and loaded, sails were folded, sails were raised, fishermen coming, fishermen leaving. The women waiting patiently, their legs dangling over the side of the jetty. I smiled inwardly when I knew: I would try fishing, but this time as boss.

What did I know about Caribbean fishing? I had had some experience in Alaska, and I had just spent three hours sitting in the sun drinking rum with two Miskito Indian lobster divers who explained in drunken detail how to trap lobster and make a lot of money. What more did I need to know? Even as drunk and content as I was I knew that the answer was a lot, maybe too much. But I would learn, people can learn.

I would have to find a boat. The money I had left from selling gold was very little. 'Would it be enough?' I asked my two drinking companions.

'*Si, amigo*, plenty, even enough for another bottle, maybe two,' they drunkenly replied, howling with laughter.

A boat was never found, a boat was built. Thirty-two foot long and eleven wide. A gaff-rigged sloop, built by local hands from local wood. A strong boat made for hard work. We painted the hull black, the gunnels gold, the mast was teak, the sails maroon. We painted the face of a beautiful woman on her bow and called her the *Creole Princess*.

I chose three men as the main crew. Moses, a lean, tightly-muscled Creole who lived on coffee and cigarettes, was my rudder man. He had spent twenty years sailing the coast, but always as rudder man of somebody else's boat. Moses drank, and when he drank, he listened to no one. I was told that you couldn't get him out to sea when his mood was not just right, but that he was one of the best boatmen around when his mood was. I knew I was taking a risk, and I expected trouble from him, but from the beginning he and his brother José had watched out for me. They had made sure I was not cheated, they drank with me and protected me. That was enough reason to give him a chance.

José was the sail man. Like Moses, José had fought as a Contra during the war against the Sandinista government. He had been a *commandante*, a leader of sixty men. People said he was a fierce fighter. His body was scarred with bullet and shrapnel wounds. José was almost fifty, but as agile as a deer. He knew as much about catching fish as anyone on the coast. Against the wishes of both José and Moses, who preferred working only with family, Artillio, a dark-skinned Indian, was given the job of main hand. Like the brothers, he had been a Contra. Artillio's war duties included running a small open boat along the coast supplying the bush fighters with ammunition and food. He knew the coast and he could fish, and that was important to me.

Our first trip was to hunt snook, a flat-nosed fish that grew to fifteen pounds and spawned in the lagoons that bite into the otherwise flat and unremarkable Nicaraguan coast. We were going to fish them with seine nets from the beach, and with gill nets from a few hundred metres out. We planned on working twenty hours a day. We would need six more men. We found them on the jetty and the beach. In a town so poor working men come easy.

The supplies had to be bought. Flour and rice, coffee, sugar, almost more sugar than rice. A root vegetable called uka, banana, breadfruit – that should keep us healthy. Diesel, line, hooks, knives, lamps, kerosene, bullets – nobody travels without bullets on the Mosquito Coast. I expected the preparations to take four days; we needed eight. Artillio was invaluable, he knew where to buy and how much to pay.

The supplies had to be carried to the *Creole Princess*. Moses and José gave no help: they were resting. On the Mosquito Coast the rudder and sail man were never expected to ready a boat. The rest of the hired crew were also of no help, but in their case it was not so much tradition as too much rum. Artillio and I did the work alone. Artillio's strength was essential. A small man who seemed to be composed entirely of muscle, he made up for the missing men.

The *Creole Princess* was not launched at the jetty, but in the tiny harbour of a small village called Lamlaya. In Lamlaya it was protected from the seas and wind, as all new-born boats should be.

Lamlaya reclined at the edge of an estuary created by the powerful Wawa River flowing into the sea. It languished (Lamlaya was a languishing type of village, as well as a reclining one), seven kilometres inland from Puerto Cabezas and two hours' sailing to the sea. The road to Lamlaya was as unloved as the town itself. The deep ruts gouged into it by driving rain were never repaired, and in most places you needed a four-wheel drive to push your way through the mud. At times it was impassable.

Back in Puerto Cabezas, I found the crew in a bar near the jetty. We collected José and Moses from their homes by the beach. Only the ice that would keep our fish from rotting had to be bought from the fish factory and loaded. We were ready. We drove back to Lamlaya, to the *Creole Princess*, the ice bags piled high on the flatbed truck, our men clinging drunkenly to the sideboards.

Lamlaya is not so much a town as a graveyard for old boats. Its harbour is filled with ancient fishing trawlers, broken hulks, even a rusting landing craft, a reminder of the days when the narrow waterways could float the biggest vessels. The small wooden houses that frame the harbour on one side have been converted into shops and simple restaurants, places to eat or get drunk. All are built on stilts, a protection from the high tides that can drown you in your kitchen if you build too low. At night, candles light the town. There is no electricity.

The *Creole Princess* was floating, waiting, the men were aboard, the motor was primed with gasoline and started.

'Slack that rope yonder,' yelled Moses in his lilting Creole accent, and we were gliding away.

Floating down the estuary fills you with a sense of calm, contentment, confidence. The water biting its way through the thick mangrove is gentle and inviting. This changes quickly when the boat rounds the last turn in the river, moments before it drives into the sea.

On our left side, a white sand beach appeared, running endlessly along the coast towards our destination in the north. On our right stood the village of Waw Waw, small wooden houses standing on long legs, looking seaward. Tall coconut palms bent like old men who had to carry too much through their lives crowded the spaces between the huts. The villagers gathered amongst the grazing cattle and watched.

To enter the sea we had to cross a bar. Artillio, who had crossed many bars during his gun-running days for the Contras, explained it to me carefully many times. 'A place where river meets sea,' he would begin, 'this meeting creates a build-up of sand that fills in the river mouth, causing shallows. There is, however, almost always a deep channel gouged by the racing currents running through this sand. Depending on the tide and the weather, the channel and the surrounding water can be as calm as a backyard pond full of ornamental fish, but at other times waves ride over the shallows like wild horses crossing a small stream. Terrifying.' Today was terrifying.

The first wave swept over the bow. I felt confident. This boat could take it. But when the waves started to swamp us from the sides my confidence ebbed away. The sea started to swirl around us, buffeting us, drenching us, frightening us, but through we sailed. The *Creole Princess* had been well built.

Once across the bar we steered her north towards the fishing grounds. Past Puerto Cabezas with its long jetty protruding like the tongue of a rude child, past Tuapi, and still further to Krukira, a village that nestles far inland on the edge of a lagoon, hidden from view.

We had been travelling eight hours when the cry came for food. We had supplies to last us ten days, but there was no meat. We would have to catch fish. The anchor was dropped, the fishing canoe hurled over the side, the net loaded. Eight men piled in. We headed through the choppy surf towards the beach.

We were seine fishing: one end of our net was thrown from the canoe, four men clambered from the boat in chest high water.

'Haul the end,' yelled José the sail man, who was fast gaining a reputation as José the tyrant. The canoe moved off, trailing the net in a semicircle. The four men still remaining beached and anchored the canoe high on the sand. Out they jumped. The loose end of the net was taken up and the two groups started to walk towards each other, heaving and straining, pulling the net towards shore. 'Hold the bottom of the net to the ground, pull, pull.' We would catch the fish in a purse in the middle of the net.

Artillio was left behind to guard the *Creole*, but something was wrong. He was waving his hands frantically. Now we could see it as well. A boat was crossing the Krukira bar, travelling fast. It had almost reached the *Creole Princess* before it became clear that it was carrying only men. We leaped back into our own canoe, our net was quickly retrieved and stored. '*Wap, wap*,' (let's go, let's go) everyone screamed as we headed through the breakers, driving hard for the *Creole Princess*.

We arrived to find Artillio standing on the bow of the boat, balancing lightly, his left hand wrapped around a wire stay that supported the mast, his right hand balled into a fist striking at the air. He was arguing passionately with the men from Krukira who seemed not to be listening as they stood whispering to each other, building up courage. Artillio was doing his best to reply to accusations shouted out by a small man with a wide scar that ran across his neck and disappeared into his discoloured blue T-shirt. No, we were not fishing in their territory, yes we would soon leave, yes we had respect for their community. None of these answers seemed to make much difference, their leader was not going to be convinced, dialogue was not his passion. As the Krukira Indians stood screaming insults and threats José moved to my left. He had heard enough, out came his machete. The nose of our boat dipped gently towards the water as our men, who had been standing grouped together on the iceboxes in the guts of the *Creole Princess*, moved forward as one towards the Krukira boat. They saw we were ready to fight.

As they sped off they screamed more threats and obscenities, but these were barely heard as the wind carried them away. Relief came to everybody, the warrior instinct had passed. We all agreed that it was foolish to fight over fish, especially when we had caught so few.

Further north we sailed, three hours more until we finally came to another bar, Awastara's bar. Awastara's bar can be passed only at high tide, and then only in a smaller boat than the *Creole Princess*. Overboard into the confused water went our canoe. We would have to ride over the surf to the beach, manhandle our boat across the sand, and set her once again in the water of a narrow channel that would take us to a small bay thirty minutes' paddling away.

This trip was necessary because we needed to make an agreement with the people of Awastara. It was their territory, it would be their fish we would catch. We couldn't afford disputes, confrontation, enemies. We only wanted to earn a living.

As we rounded yet another twist in a canal of endless twists, a lagoon appeared. Strong slender fishing dories were anchored in no particular order. Red boats with blue piping, yellow with red piping, their names roughly painted on the side – *Coolcat*, *Sea Wind*, *Shady Lady* – more than I could count filling the half moon of water. This was the fleet of Awastara: boats used to hunt turtle, lobster, fish, to transport goods, sometimes to carry pirates.

The lagoon was edged by mudflats, which in turn led to swamps. It was through the swamps we sloshed towards the village a mile away.

Awastara is spread out: Miskitos like space. The sea forces them together, working as a team against the dangers, but on land they prefer more isolation. Their sparsely furnished houses were built high, and linked only by water-drowned trails. Horses graze alongside foraging pigs. Why, I wondered, did they need horses?

'To ride!' yelled José, exasperated, 'these people are cowboy sailors.'

We headed for the house of the mayor, the most powerful

person in the community. He was the man who settled the disagreements, disputes. In this completely isolated community with no police force, he was the law. He governed with the help of an elected council and a group of elders, but his power was supreme. We needed him on our side.

'Would we be allowed to fish, could the council judge?' we asked. He agreed, a bell rang, people started drifting slowly towards the village clinic. The clinic had no nurses, no medicines, its windows had been broken and the inside was used as a communal toilet.

'It was built with development money,' José explained. 'Mon, they build the clinic then they steal the rest of the money. There is nothing left over to pay nurses with or to buy medicines.'

'Who does?' I asked.

'Anybody who is lucky enough to get control of the money,' he answered, 'the president of the country, the governor of the region, the mayor of the village, anybody who is lucky.'

'Would you,' I asked, 'cheat your own people?'

'Cheat who?' he replied. 'The development people come here to spend other people's money. They're paid well, it makes them feel very important, a good person. What they bring or build we've never had, mostly never needed, and when they leave, well . . . their buildings just rot away and collapse and the agricultural projects dry and shrivel, but we go on, just like always. So you see,' he went on patiently, 'no one is cheated. Some people just have more luck than others.'

The villagers gathered in a circle outside the building. Old men clustered together on one side. These were the council of elders, traditionally a strong group in Miskito society. The council members, younger and harder to recognize, took their place amongst the rest of the villagers. José explained to me that it all depended on the decision of the council, but they were greatly influenced by the feelings of the village people, and more so by the village elders, and in this village in particular, the mayor. It would not be easy.

The council had other problems that had to be solved first. Ours was not pressing. A young drug addict was pushed forward, limping badly from an infected foot – the result of a dirty needle. His hair had fallen out, he looked pale, weakened, sick. They all milled around him yelling their accusations, pointing, shoving. It was agreed that the boy was a thief, the villagers would do nothing more to help him, he would be sent to jail in Puerto Cabezas.

Now it was our turn. It had been decided that José would speak for us. Actually he had decided he would speak for us. He did so eloquently, embracing the part, moving around the circle of men, gesturing expansively as he spoke. José offered to pay ten per cent of our fish catch to the village as well as allowing the Awastara people to carry off any undersized fish in our seine net. A contract was agreed and, for my benefit, written up in Spanish. Now we could fish.

If we hurried we could make it to the *Creole Princess* before dark. Through the swamp we trotted, reaching the lagoon just as the sun fell. Sandfly hour, the biting hour, the time when you could be driven mad by swarms of small black insects that lived on your blood and never stopped feasting until they were gorged. But they were never gorged.

We knew something was wrong before we reached the mudflats. There was no long shape, no shadow in the mud: our canoe had been stolen.

That evening we slept in the house of a village elder. I was given the only bed. The next day we recovered the canoe, it had been left in the mangroves halfway along the canal.

'Kids,' they said, 'they needed transport to reach the beach.'

'Why would they want to go there?' I asked.

José answered, 'Cocaine, it washes ashore all the time, people running it from Columbia to the north, boxes of it.' He smiled deeply, 'Finding one of them would be much better than being in charge of development money.'

The *Creole Princess* rode lightly on the waves as we approached. It was late in the morning and the sun had already begun to scorch the decks. The men had waited patiently for us to return with the contract. They were accustomed to waiting. On the beach people from the village had gathered in anticipation, today they would eat the fish that we would catch for them. Our canoe was again thrown overboard and loaded with the seine net, our men followed.

We worked the beaches each morning for the next seven days, blistering our hands on the seine rope, and roasting our salt-smothered bodies under a relentless sun. In the beginning, the village people helped us pull, but soon lost interest and contented themselves with poking through the net with sticks trying to separate the edible fish from the sting rays or small spiked catfish that speared and poisoned you when you brushed against them.

Our agreement was that they take the un-sellable or undersized fish from our net, but often they picked out the large snook that earned us our living. Sometimes there were squabbles over fish rights, not only between them and us, but also amongst themselves. At times I was afraid there would be trouble, all men carried machetes, and many carried guns, but calm was always restored.

We piled our catch on the beach and covered it with branches and leaves to protect it from the sun and vultures until we were ready to return to the *Creole Princess*. We buried the small catfish in shallow graves so that their spikes couldn't poison the barefooted villagers. The masses of waste fish were left to suffocate slowly under the full sun, on the scorching sand. The sea birds waited until we had left.

When the tide turned, the snook moved to deeper water and we would return to our princess to gut and clean and eat our first meal of the day, always fish. Often it was past midday. If the weather had turned bad, the sea would turn rough, and our fish would be tied securely in sacks and fastened to the canoe before we paddled back. Sometimes we were swamped, but our canoe always floated, and our fish was always safe.

We set our gill nets perpendicular to the beach, trapping the large snook as they patrolled the shore looking for shrimp. This net had to be checked every four hours night and day, good weather and foul. Dead fish turn bad very quickly when left in water. The men slept on the open deck, on top of the iceboxes, wrapped in tarpaulin and sail.

On the seventh day we were forced to leave. Our ice was melting, our fish would rot. One of our men needed a doctor: he had been speared three times by a catfish, his leg was swollen and bled continuously.

As we pulled anchor and headed south, I could see a 'squall', a tropical storm, building, blackening the sky. The violent winds and thundering rain that it would bring meant we would have to lower the main sail until it passed. I exchanged a smile with José.

'Mon, this place only lets you take it easy when you're dead,' he screamed over the noise of the wind as he worked to loosen ropes that had become entangled in our seine net. The rest of the men hauled down the sails, yelling with delight, the rain already stinging their excited faces. All that was lying loose was tied down, or stored below.

We watched the storm tearing up the sea, moving nearer and nearer. We felt the *Creole Princess* begin to heave and roll. Soon the storm would fall on us. The men held tight, and calmly smoked. We were ready.

PAPA TARA

We could see it only as a spot, a blemish on the near perfect horizon, a small dark stain on a calm tropical sea. As we sailed nearer it took a shape, but an unrecognizable one. It was surrounded by rock and reef, giving it protection from the deep waters. Closer, closer we came. Now we could see it clearly, but we still couldn't make out what it was.

We were thirty miles from the coast and sixty out of our home port of Puerto Cabezas in north-eastern Nicaragua. We were travelling to the fishing grounds on the Misquito Keys, an area of shallow ocean where the seabed is formed by deep canyons and high ridges. In some places the ridges push to the surface as if looking for breath and become small islands. These are quickly covered with mangrove bush and become home to sandflies and mosquitoes. They are inhospitable, almost impassable. There are coral reefs that nourish species of fish whose brightness and brilliance remind you of fireworks exploding, colour upon colour, and there are barren rocky outcroppings waiting to rip the bottom out of anything that thinks it might pass, like a heated iron peeling away flesh. But if you are careful and travel only by day, always watching closely, you can pass between these dangers, or around them, and then you come to a place where red snapper and yellowtail fish jump right into your boat, and lobster crawl up your anchor line and surrender. Or so I had been told.

As we lowered our sails and started our small outboard motor to manoeuvre the *Creole Princess* around the shallows and between the jagged rocks, I finally understood that I was looking at a house. A small blue-and-red house that had been built on a platform laid across and fastened to three narrow fishing canoes. The platform was wide enough to allow you to walk around the building and to run a business from it. It was a lobster-buying house. This floating building was moored by four ropes fastened to poles driven into the shallow water. Those ropes and the surrounding shoals were all that stopped this house boat, the *Papa Tara*, from being driven by wind or tide far out into the Caribbean or, worse, towards destruction on the Nicaraguan coast.

As we tied up alongside the *Papa Tara* we were greeted by a large unshaven man in shorts and sandals. His skin – burnt bright pink from the sun – warned us that he wasn't a local. His deep, rasping voice sounded like his vocal cords had been notched.

'I'm Norman Strattford,' he screamed to me above the noise of the compressor that roared in the background. 'How the fuck are ya?'

We were dropping off some ice to Norman on our way out to the fishing grounds. His wife Sylvia normally carried it in their launch, but the engine had stopped working again and they were desperate: without ice the lobster would rot.

My crew knew him well, and José, who had worked for Norman once and liked to talk, made sure during our journey that I shared all their information.

'Skipper,' he began, 'he likes to drink, and when he drinks he drinks a lot. If you are with him when he is drunk, don't,' and he repeated 'don't' two more times while striking his closed fist on the icebox, 'make him mad.'

'*Porque?*' asked Artillio, who spoke only a little Creole but understood much more.

'Because he will knock your little Indian head in if you do.'

'Just Indian heads?' I asked, trying not to smile.

José looked directly at me, trying to convince himself that it was a serious question, and lifted his face skywards as if wondering how God could produce so many fools. 'Norman Strattford ain't no racist,' he screamed, 'It don't matter to him whether it's Indian like Artillio's, black like mine, or just a plain white head like yours. I seen Norman completely wreck bars. He break the chairs, everything, just like a cowboy, and then beats up them little policemen they send to capture him. And then, when they do get him to jail, and it takes about all the lawmen in town, he beats up the other prisoners, mostly just drunk lobster divers who would be beating up on each other anyway, so they have to give him a private cell. They hate capturing Norman Strattford.'

'He's a bad man then?' I asked.

'No!' yelled José, becoming more and more exasperated with my questions. 'Just don't make him mad.' Artillio had made sweet black coffee, Moses was at the tiller and the sails were nicely set. The *Creole Princess* caressed the light waves. José settled his back against the mast, lit his own cigarette and then my cigar as he always insisted on doing. 'You waste too many of them damn matches,' he always told me, ignoring me when I pointed out that I bought the damn matches in the first place, and continued his story. 'As far as I remember, I saw him for the first time about four years ago, it was not long after the war finished. I heard that he had been a soldier in England.'

'He's English?'

Jose nodded as if it were common knowledge.

Still considering this new piece of information, I asked, 'A soldier like you?'

'I was a bush fighter, I didn't salute anybody,' Jose sneered. 'When I knew him he was in business with his brother on a fishing boat in Honduras. They came down this way because you could fish anything all year round, no rules. There were problems with money, the boat broke, it wasn't paid for, his brother cheated him. Mon, he even had a plane at that time but had to sell it to pay off the debts.'

'What did he do to his brother?'

'Beat the hell out of him.'

'What would you have done, José?' I asked.

'Me, I would have been plenty vexed, I'd have killed him.'

'And then?'

'And then nothing, just a lot of drinking, a lot of fighting. He had nowhere to go.'

'But then he met Sylvia?'

'Yes mon, then he met Sylvia.'

I had met Sylvia myself in town a few days before we started our trip. I had gone to her house to arrange the business of transporting Norman's ice. Sylvia was very short with enormous breasts resting on a considerable stomach. Her arse was large. She wore shorts and a tank top which left her half-naked. Her grin was wide, but her teeth were not complete. She was Creole like José and Moses, but blacker, a clouded-night black. Her skin was smooth and shining. She was very beautiful.

Sylvia was not paying me to deliver the goods; on the coast you helped each other. But she did insist on buying me a drink, and over eight beers and half a bottle of rum in a bar built on a high bank just above the tideline I learned how she and Norman had met.

'You see that woman?'

I looked towards a girl wearing a very short frayed cotton dress and sitting on the lap of a very drunk Indian diver who seemed to be more interested in not falling from his stool than he was in the woman.

'She's a whore. Don't get me wrong, I'm not looking down my nose at her, I ain't no virgin, but I ain't never had to do what she does. But I would have if that was the only way to feed my children. They's sea whores. They usually travel in pairs, two girls and a paddler. They work the shrimp boats anchored off the coast. Sometimes they travel five miles out in them leaking canoes to whore for the crews, sometimes they get caught in them squalls. No, I ain't never had to do that. When the boats are further out or the weather's too bad they hang out in the bars, at least it's dry.'

Sylvia could drink as much as anybody I had ever met. Beer was always washed down with rum, and then rum with beer. She wore more gold rings, earrings and necklaces than anyone else in Puerto. When I asked if it was safe to do so in such a poor country she simply opened her purse: nestled between perfume and bank notes was a Makarov, a Russian pistol. 'Ain't nobody taking what I got,' was all she said.

'I've been so fucking poor I sold ice on streets to feed my kids. Ice that I begged from the fish factory. That's when I meet Norman and then I had him to support too.' She gave me a wink, 'You'd think once you found a gringo your troubles would be solved. He was in a bad way then, didn't have no money neither, we lived off that ice for a year and when we found a little extra Norman would go on one of his drinking sprees, and often enough he'd end up in jail.

'One time I got this work on a shrimp boat as cook and I left him locked up for two weeks. He done started begging me in the end to get him out. That slowed him down for quite a while. Can you imagine, two weeks in that stinking filth, one small window and sometimes twelve men to a room, and the noise: them outlaws howl like wild dogs. Only eating rice and beans, no cigarettes, no beers.' She howled with laughter from the thought. 'He deserved it.

'Sometimes when he was real drunk he would pick me up like a baby and carry me home. He couldn't do it now, I'm too fat, and besides I hardly ever let him get off that little boat and come to town.'

I walked unsteadily to the bar and bought two more beers. The girl serving had run out of change and paid me in Chiclet gum, a local custom. She smiled sweetly and ran her hand along the length of my forearm, feeling my thick blond hair. 'I'm better than Sylvia,' she whispered.

'And I'm a poor gringo,' I whispered back.

'Isn't no such thing,' she replied, forming her mouth into an O shape and pushing her tongue through the opening.

The jukebox played scratchy country music and the drunks, mostly Miskito Indians from villages along the coast, became drunker. Some sank into a stupor while others sat brooding. One of them crashed heavily to the floor but Sylvia took no notice. 'In the end we had some luck. We made a deal with one of the fish factories. They paid for the building of the *Papa Tara*. They gave us a compressor to fill the diving tanks that the Indians use, a big old launch with three leaks to haul the product back to Puerto, a motor that breaks about every trip, and they gave us a couple of iceboxes and a little money to buy our first supplies. And we agreed to sit out in the middle of the ocean and buy lobster for them. I know they only done it because Norman was a gringo, don't matter how far you fall if you're a gringo people still believe in you. In this case they was right, because that darn Norman is a good honest man.'

As I stepped aboard the *Papa Tara* Norman handed me a cold beer and then quickly left to unload the ice and supplies we had carried for him. We had arrived in the late afternoon, the *Papa Tara* was half in shadow, and the diving boats had just returned with their catch. Norman was weighing and buying amidst chaos.

The lobster needed to be hauled up, the sails to be lowered and stored, the boats tied off, the tanks moved onto the *Papa Tara* and filled by the compressor that roared and roared. Divers added to the cacophony of sound as they howled with pleasure or disappointment when their catch was weighed, yelled greetings, or screamed orders.

Norman stood towering above them, pen and pad ready to methodically record every transaction. But there were still mistrust, still disputes. The Indian divers argued over what was legal size, what should be bought, and what not. Norman only paid for the full-grown animals. The *Papa Tara* listed dangerously under the weight of the commotion.

Artillio poked his head out of the *Creole Princess*'s forward cabin like a ferret sniffing for danger and cried: '*plume, plume!*' – food, food. José and Moses stopped cleaning and mending the lobster traps, I finished tying the hooks and sinkers on our fishing tackle in preparation for the morning, and we sat back comfortably to eat fish fried with garlic, a root vegetable called uka, and bread made from flour, salt and sugar. We finished with hot, sweet black coffee.

The light was almost gone as we sipped our second cup, but the movement around us had not slowed. Norman was still buying lobster and tanks were still being filled, and now, because of the darkness, a generator was adding its growl to the confusion.

I gazed to one side of the *Papa Tara* and took my first good look at the huts that had been built in a line on poles in the shallows. The framing and the floor were made from wood, but the roof and sides were covered with plastic. There were fires burning in each of the huts and rice was boiling, lobster frying. Old men sat worrying the pans, mothering the food. Moses noticed my interest and explained that Norman had built the huts to attract the divers.

'Not much,' I answered.

'Shit you gringos are spoiled,' sniggered José. 'Where would you rather sleep, in one of them huts or in the fishing dory wrapped in the sail?'

I could see his point. 'How many men are working here?' I asked.

'How many boats you see?' replied Moses, who always had time for questions that José thought not worth his consideration. I looked about and saw that there were sail dories tied off on two sides of the *Papa Tara* and more were anchored in front of the huts. Divers, wearing only shorts, their skin darkened and their hair wild and unkempt, bleached and streaked by salt and sun, busied themselves checking their tanks, mending the sail ropes or the leaks, or just sharpening the knives that they all carried to slice the upper part of the lobster from the tail. Norman only bought tails.

I counted carefully. 'Ten,' I answered.

'Right,' said Moses, 'they carry about five divers per boat and all them boys need helpers because they don't dive from the sail dory, they work from those little paddle canoes they got tied over there to one of them huts, and they need someone to stay in the canoe and paddle above where they're working. Sometimes them little paddle boys lose their divers and when he comes up there ain't no boat to crawl back into. And then he's shark bait. Then there's the captain of the sail dory who don't do much except collect his money for being the boat owner. That's eleven people times ten boats, that's one hundred and ten people. Plus they always bring some kids along for the ride. Them old men have got to cook for plenty of people and them divers are always powerful hungry.

And,' he continued, wagging a scarred finger to emphasize the point, 'they have to carry all the firewood and fresh water from their village on the coast.'

'What about the food?'

'Well they get that from Norman, he takes it out of their catch.'

'Company prices?' I asked.

'Yeah, but that Norman he's a fair man, he don't rob no Indian. And anyway they mostly eat lobster and rice.'

It was late in the night before I got a chance to talk to Norman. By the time he had washed and iced the catch, filled the air tanks and cleared his boat of customers and layabouts all my crew were sleeping. We were alone. We settled with our backs against the wall, the generator still growled next to us, but after the noise made by Indians and compressor, it almost seemed quiet.

'These people drive me fucking crazy,' he began, 'always arguing and fighting, trying some sort of con, breaking my boat. But you know, sometimes I visit their village to collect water or help them carry wood, and I'm treated like a king. They're really good people, just fucking noisy. I heard on the radio,' he continued, 'that you talked to Sylvia.'

'Yeah,' I replied, 'but by the end of the night she had me so drunk I couldn't talk to anyone.'

'Yeah, that's my Sylvia, she's fucking something ain't she? That's a woman with no fear. You know she used to be married to a preacher?'

'She never said,' I answered, taking another sip of beer and letting the alcohol conquer my tired body.

'She had two kids with the motherfucker. They lived in a village at the mouth of the Rio Coco. He used to beat the fuck out of her. She told me she stayed with him so long for the kids, but in the end she had to leave or she would have killed him. I know she was telling me the truth. After that she started working with lobster divers from Sandy Bay as cook. Sometimes I see them boys and they tell me stories about her. They say that she was good at smelling out shallow water,' he grinned and looked at me sideways. 'I bet you didn't know you could smell out shallow water, did you? It's all that algae growing on the rocks. Anyway, they used to sit her in the bow of the boat when they travelled at night, crazy Indians travelling at night in these waters. She smelled so good they called her dog in the end. Come up here, dog, they would call to her when they weren't sure. They really loved my Sylvia.'

A strong breeze had picked up, lifting the water and forcing the waves to skip and hop over the exposed rocks.

The beer was working pretty good now and when he continued his story it was with a sharp melancholic edge. 'I've been out here six months. That little Sylvia she don't like me coming to town too much. I suppose you already heard I can make some trouble.' I said nothing, he didn't expect an answer. 'I get a bit lonely sometimes, especially when the divers have left, but at least we're back on our feet again, both of us.' He never mentioned selling ice, neither did I.

Suddenly he heaved himself heavily to his feet, lit another cigarette and pointed to the waves. 'Some fucking times it's all white out there, the waves try to crush, roll or drown anything floating, the winds howl and drive rain and storm blackness towards you so fast that you lose your way in minutes, and my Sylvia makes the sixty-mile trip out here two, sometimes three times a week. She can't swim, she doesn't carry life jackets, she has no radio. She's the maddest, bravest thing on this coast.

'One time that great fucking motor they give her broke down and she floated onto the shore, it was two days before a boat come along and picked her up. Luckily it was good weather when it broke, otherwise she would have been swamped for sure.'

There weren't many Englishmen in this part of the world; I asked him what he had done before. 'Not much,' he replied. 'I'm a drifter, I was in the army for a while, a good while. I made sergeant but a man gets sick of being told what to do all the time. Then I bought a plane ticket to Jamaica, always wanted to see it. In them days it was beautiful, people were friendly, drugs weren't a problem. I got a job on a sugar plantation, best life a man ever had, and you know I like black women. Then I got restless again and found myself a job with a big timber company in the States, made pretty good money, learned how to fly, bought a plane, and then made the worst decision of my life.'

'Your brother?' I said.

'Yeah, my fucking brother. I see you've already heard.'

It had become late and tiredness overtook us. Norman switched the generator off and the stillness was overwhelming. We slept.

'*Ouwwaa, ouwwaa . . . Ouw, ouw,* reckon them damn divers are awake,' said José to no one in particular, 'when them awake everybody has got to get up.'

You could barely make out their boats in the pre-dawn light. Their bright colours were muted and dull, men were stirring everywhere you looked, splashing cool seawater on their heads to wash away the sleep, pissing or shitting over the side of their boats. In the huts the fires had been long lit, the rice almost ready.

The sun had barely risen when the first boat glided away on the glass-smooth water, a whiff of breeze barely fattening its sail. Then the next, until the last had carried its men to the sea.

We moved more slowly, but not long after the last dory had passed by we had raised our sails and were heading towards our fishing grounds twenty-five miles to the north-east. We anchored in about twenty metres of water, twelve miles off the largest island in the Keys. Now it was time for Artillio to desert his kitchen. He was also our lobster man.

We carried sixty traps, not that many, but the *Creole Princess* had just been built and this was one of our first trips. If all went well we planned to fish two hundred. The traps were made from wood and bamboo, the base filled with cement to give it weight. They were covered with chicken wire, an entrance had been made for the lobster to crawl through.

We used cowhide as bait. It had been lying in the bowels of our boat the whole trip and was now stinking and maggot-infested. Artillio was the only man who could stomach it. He cut and baited all sixty traps, retching the whole time, but never stopping. We could only watch from a distance.

The traps weighed fourteen kilos. Each was tied individually to a main line by lengths of rope. They were spaced two metres apart and heaved overboard in sets of ten. A float was fastened to the end of the main line. Artillio bestowed a kiss on each trap as it was dropped into the water and whispered 'lobster'. We had problems with tangled ropes, broken traps that had to be mended and in the end it took us the whole day to get them into the sea. We had not eaten, we were exhausted, but we knew if we caught lobster, we would be rich.

The lobster traps had to be left for at least four days. Now it was time to fish. Before the Caribbean darkness blinded us and made travel risky we raised the sails and moved closer to the island.

It was still dark when I heard José shuffling about, spitting, lighting his first cigarette. The light from his torch punched at the blackness as he searched for his fishing bag, Moses followed. Soon both were calling for coffee. Artillio swore quietly, primed and lit the gas lamp and stumbled out onto the cluttered deck to bring fresh water from one of the plastic containers. The aroma of coffee and the heat from the gas stove mingled, melting the edge of the morning cold, leaving us tasting the coffee before it had been poured.

José's line had barely touched the water when he felt strong tugs. That meant snapper biting. Each hand line was tied with two hooks, we carried shrimp and mullet to use as bait, and the fish were hungry. We were pulling red snapper and yellowtail almost as fast as our sinkers settled on the seabed. Two- and three-pound fish fought our lines constantly, sometimes two on the same line: battling, running, slowing down, then running again until their heads broke the surface, and then still they fought. Sometimes they would win, sacrificing a piece of lip or a gill if the hook was deep, but they would survive.

In two hours we had sixty pounds of fish dying on the bottom of the boat, sucking at the air and gulping for breath. Their clear eyes were dull and blood from their wounds mingled with the water that seeped in through the hull. And then suddenly nothing. I turned to José looking for an answer but he was already pulling heavy line out of his fishing bag and tying on a large strong hook. Moses and Artillio began pulling their lines in. I knew then that something big, a hunter, had startled the fish.

José pulled a small yellowtail that had just been caught from the bottom of the boat and pierced its tail with his hook. He hurled it over the side as living bait.

You could see the strike clearly just below the surface. It was a barracuda. It moved in so fast that you could barely follow it. The barracuda devoured the bait without seeming to slow down. José reefed on his line hard but lost balance and stumbled backwards. The barracuda had taken a great chunk from the fish but had missed the hook and escaped. Moses had already grabbed a small snapper from the bottom of the boat ready to bait José's line when he pulled in.

The second fish was much more lively and gave the barracuda

a chase, but it had no chance; it was already dying from the hook. When the barracuda bit, José had him. But this was no snapper. He ran with the hook and dived – sometimes the line would go slack as he raced to the surface – but then he would hit again and make José close his eyes in pain. He sped under the boat and around the outboard motor. José had to change positions repeatedly, crawling over the nets from one side of the *Creole Princess* to the other, the line held high over his head so as not to tangle it on the deck. When he finally pulled the barracuda to the surface his hands had been sliced open.

Moses called to me to grab the club, I brought it down twice on the barracuda's head before he was stunned enough to lift into the boat. Bleeding from the mouth and from his head wound he wriggled, constantly looking for an enemy, scattering the other fish, not wanting to die. I clubbed him again and again until we could come close enough to take the hook out. We did this carefully, his deep mouth was filled with long sharp teeth that could rip you open and force you to return home, and nobody could afford that.

We fished till the sun set and then we began to clean our catch by the light of our kerosene lamps. In the dim light our hands were spiked constantly by the sharp fins or by the rough bones as we hauled out the guts. Sea salt bit into our wounds.

While Moses, Jose and I cleaned the fish, Artillio would cook. He would take as many of the newly gutted fish as he thought would satisfy us, slice them on their sides, rub in salt, and then pack in pieces of freshly cut garlic, coat the fish in flour and then fry them.

We fished for four days, constantly moving, hunting. On the morning of the fourth day we lifted our anchor and headed back to check our lobster traps. We had iced about three hundred pounds of sellable catch. We were making a living.

The wind had picked up, and we raised the yankee. The *Creole Princess* was leaning deeply into the choppy sea, punching through the waves, enjoying herself.

José saw them first, they were anchored close in to one of the mangrove islands, nestling into the foliage. Their boat was long and narrow, fast, and you could clearly count the eight men hunched down, cowering from the wind. They had not expected to see us. 'Drug runners,' pronounced José, 'Colombian.'

Their motor started and they came towards us, catching us easily. As they pulled alongside Jose pointed out the AK47s lying on the bottom of their boat. They greeted us in Miskito. They were not Colombian after all. A man with a full black beard stood holding the motor handle, balancing easily, in charge. What were we doing here, he wanted to know.

'Fishing, just fishing,' answered José, gesturing to our iceboxes.

'No traps,'

'No traps,' answered José. The bearded man nodded, said more things to José that I could not understand, and then demanded enough fish to feed his crew. Before they left they sped around the *Creole Princess* twice, smiling.

'What was that about?' I asked, furious that my Miskito was still so bad. José spat before he answered, 'Them Indian boys don't want anybody out here hunting their lobster, their fucking lobster they say. That was Pernello, I fight with him in the war, he was a back-shooter then and still is. Now he the leader of all them bad boys from Sandy Bay Village. They say this is their area and nobody hunts lobster without their permission. Them damn Indians, who he think he is, this sea belongs to all the people of Nicaragua.'

'What did you answer, José?'

'What you expect me to answer, them with eight guns and us with only one. We're just fishing.'

201

We pulled our traps as quickly as possible, constantly on guard for the Sandy Bay boys. It took two men to haul up and two more to drag them onto the boat, to stack and lash them down. The sea was choppy and the boat rolled constantly. Our traps had come up mostly empty, the weather was changing, Pernello had made our mood black.

Afterwards, we anchored in shallower water east of the largest mangrove island Cayos Misquitos, and continued fishing. It was there that the storm caught us.

The wind had been building all evening but it wasn't until after midnight that the *Creole Princess*, which until then had been pointing into the weather, riding the waves, lifting and descending as elegantly as a child's plastic toy in a restless bath, started to bang head first, hard into the troughs, each descent wrenching her hull. She began to retreat. The storm had wrestled our anchor loose and we were moving aimlessly in an ocean filled with madness. Moses started the motor but our stern was often so far out of the water that the propellor, screaming and roaring in protest, had only air to bite into.

Slowly we moved through the blackness towards the island, Artillio in the bow searching, listening, smelling for shallows, while the rest of us huddled in the back trying to give weight to the stern, forcing the motor into the water.

We were moving across the waves and the wind, our gunwales constantly pushed deep into the water by the sea rolling over our side. Each wave forcing us to hold on grimly.

Over the screech of the wind we heard a snap, our mast had cracked at the top. If the top broke off it would bring all our stays down and then the whole mast would follow. José took some heavy wire and shimmied up the swaying six-metre pole. Swearing and cursing he managed to wrap the wire around the crack, binding it. It took fifteen minutes. José was almost fifty, the oldest man on the boat, we could only hold tightly and watch him sway.

Four hours later we anchored, snuggling close against the edge of the Cayos Misquitos, safe from the sea. It was so dark we had almost motored past the island into nothing.

Norman stood waiting for us as we sailed closer, his arms folded across his large bare chest. There were no boats, no old men shuffling around in the cooking huts. The divers had returned to their village the day before. Now it was quiet.

'How did you do?' he asked as he gave me his hand to help me step aboard the *Papa Tara*.

'Fair,' I replied.

'Good,' yelled José from the back of the *Creole Princess* where he had already started to clean off the decks and re-stack the traps that had come loose and moved during the storm. 'You gringos are never satisfied. Only that damn Pernello gunna give us problems in the future.'

Moses and Artillio tied the *Creole Princess* off, finished wrapping the sails, and then came to sit with us on the *Papa Tara*. Norman opened four cold beers, passed them out, and then turned and spat thickly into the water, 'So you ran into the motherfucker too.'

'Why?' I asked, 'Did you hear something else?'

'My divers told me that they hit three boats. Rodrigas, you know him?'

'Yeah, I know him,' I replied.

'Well, he was one.'

'When?'

'Three, four days ago, busted their motor, threw the lobster into the sea, tied them up and beat the hell out of them.' 'There's more,' I pushed. 'Yeah, last night after the Dakura divers left they just sped past shooting their fucking guns. I heard from some turtle hunters that slept here a few days ago that he wants to run me out. I ain't worried, my divers ain't going to let that happen, and I've got my gun,' he continued, 'that piece of shit's gunna bleed if he comes. There's no way Sylvia is going to sell ice for a living again.'

The radio began to crackle in the background, Norman rose heavily and squeezed himself into his hut. The space between his bed and the wall where the radio had been placed was just enough to allow his great bulk to manoeuvre. I could hear Sylvia's voice, she sounded worried. Norman growled back soothingly. 'She calls me when she arrives,' he offered as he sat down again next to me. 'You just missed her, she left this morning with the lobster, they finally fixed that fucking motor.'

'Is she worried?' I asked.

'Yeah, she's worried.'

We sailed away the next morning on water still irritated from the storm, under a sky filled with low grey clouds spitting light cold rain. We all sat shivering in the back of the boat. Norman stood, feet spread apart, holding onto one of the poles that held up the roof of the *Papa Tara*, bare-chested, grinning, not feeling the chill. His large frame became smaller and smaller as the *Creole Princess* moved further and further away, his smile disappearing with distance. Suddenly he roared after us that he would see us next trip, and if not, in town at Christmas.

'Christmas, that's three months away,' I called back.

'Yeah, that little Sylvia promised me time off for good behaviour. Ain't she something?'

RICKY'S CHANCE

Ricky was breathing lightly as he walked back to his corner, his gloved hands still held high as if at any moment they might be called upon to defend or attack. Blood was seeping slowly from a tiny cut above his left eye. It had mixed with his sweat, and like a new-born stream began to trickle slowly around his eyelid, before running downward over his cheekbone, flowing faster and faster until it plummeted to the ring floor beside his boot, leaving pink stains on the canvas.

As we gently unbuckled and lifted his head protector away from the cut, we could see that it was not deep, the skin had been lifted but the flesh had not opened. It wouldn't need stitches. It would heal quickly.

Ricky was one of our best professionals. A good prospect. We had been training him hard, hoping to arrange a match for him in Managua where he would have a chance to fight the best. Negotiations were in progress, but we were a long way from the capital. Ricky was unknown and we had to convince the fight promoters that he was worth the price of their plane ticket.

On the Caribbean coast of Nicaragua, in a small, corrupt,

poverty-ravaged town called Puerto Cabezas, there is a boxing gymnasium called the Puerto Cabezas Boxing Club. Between trips northward on my boat the *Creole Princess* to fish for snook and snapper, I helped to teach boxing at the club.

Our head trainer was a Nicaraguan of Spanish blood from Managua called Eduardo Sanchez. He was a small man who was always excited, unsettled and unsettling. Eduardo strutted with head held high, searching for indiscretions and screaming at anybody who moved. But he knew the fight game. His body had gone soft but he was still quick and trained fighters using rhythms and movements that fitted with the passion and excesses of the Latin character: techniques that were never taught in my country.

Our boxers were mostly Miskito Indians and English-speaking Creoles. They were a tough lot, and when they sparred they treated it like a fight. You had to be with them all the time, watching, ready to stop a killing. I believed that the time to fight hard was during a match. In training you were meant to learn. 'Protect your brains,' I always told them, 'so you can use them in the real fight when it counts.' But when their blood boiled they always forgot my advice.

We trained them on a cement floor because the bolts that held our ring together had been stolen after our last tournament. We had only a few bags to punch, a few ropes to skip, two sets of gloves to use, but it was enough.

Fighters must fight, and it had been months since we had organized a boxing tournament. Sure, every Saturday we would let the amateurs box each other. They boxed barefooted, in old shorts. They shared bloodied mouth guards and sweat-soaked gloves. The kids would swing at each other until their arms became so heavy that they couldn't raise them above their hips, then they would lean on each other, chest to chest, and pound at each other's backs. They loved it and so did the town.

But our professionals were desperate. They were fighting for a career — to fight each other on a hot Saturday afternoon meant nothing. We had to find good opponents for them and that meant we would have to fly them in from Managua, but that cost a lot of money — money we didn't have. It would be cheaper by road of course, but it was too arduous and dangerous. Nobody wanted to ride three days in a truck bumping along a dirt track, crossing broken bridges or fording swollen rivers. Nobody wanted to be robbed at gunpoint. It was that sort of trip.

Eduardo still had contacts in Managua and he was constantly trying to organize fights in the capital for our boys. When the fax arrived at the post office the word spread quickly, nothing was secret in Puerto Cabezas. They needed a one-hundred-and-twenty-eight-pound fighter. They would give Ricky a chance and fly him down, but he had to be good, he would have to fight the Nicaraguan champion. And they could use a hundred-and-fifteen-pounder in a four-rounder.

The hundred-and-fifteen-pounder would have to be Salvadore, 'The Fighting Miskito'. The problem was that he was more Salvadore, 'The Drunk Miskito' these days. We found him asleep in the market, lying on his side on top of two empty fruit crates, his elbows locked together pushing his forearms upwards towards his face, his hands cupped like a fighter's, ready even in sleep.

We had two weeks before we had to leave and each afternoon we drove them. Loosen up, warm up, skipping, shadow sparring, bag work, real sparring, then work with the *mascotes*, punching combinations, ducking, slipping, inside and rip with left, over with the right, under a hook, hook with the left, below, over the top, finish with a short right. Slowly we built up the work rate, training more rounds every day.

In the mornings when it was still blackish, when the heat was still mixed with air and the town drunks hadn't staggered as far as their homes, we would run down the beach heading south, stepping over broken bottles, leaping the ropes that anchored the dories, and ducking under the long wooden jetty. On the way we passed men pulling in the seine nets, and the fishermen who hauled the sails and readied the boats to go to sea. Everyone looked up and waved as the fighters passed. Up and back we ran, and then they would sprint, and I would cajole them. Three times a hundred metres, later five times, and still later ten. Shadowbox lightly, work on the stomach and rest.

A week before we were to leave for the fights Ricky heard that his sister had been shot dead while travelling back from Managua on one of the transport trucks that supply Puerto Cabezas with goods produced in the south. Bandits had held up the truck as it was crossing a river beside a bridge that had rotted and was too dangerous to use. There was no need to fire, the truck was moving slowly, but they fired anyway and a bullet caught Ricky's sister in the chest.

I had to buy Salvadore a pair of shoes for the trip. He took along two extra singlets, he didn't own a shirt. Ricky showed up all in white. He wore red braces that were attached to his pants and left to dangle down both sides of his legs – a fashion accessory. When I asked him about it he gave me a huge smile and answered, 'America.' He finished his ensemble with a tight, glittering, red and black waistcoat, and tiny coloured beads woven into his hair.

'*Hijo de puta*,' exclaimed Eduardo, 'Blacks gotta dress like fucking Christmas trees.'

The local television filmed us leaving. some of the boys from the gym came, and a few people from town waved us away. Salvadore kissed his wife and three children goodbye. Ricky's family, still in mourning, came to wish him luck.

The little single-engine Cessna speared forward, then rose steeply from the enormous runway that had been built during the war as a landing strip for much larger planes. It headed first towards the sea, into the wind, over the anchored shrimp boats, banked, and then turned inland to begin bouncing through the clouds towards the capital. As we approached Managua the plane crossed the large lake that bordered the city, then suddenly dived steeply, swinging sharply to the left, lining up the approach, dancing across the rooftops of the city.

Managua sprawled below us like a spreading inflamed infection; most houses were made from sheets of tin and built so close together that they seemed to be suffocating one another. They stood on bare ground, packed dirt; some people had planted banana and *platano* trees, their large green leaves shading and softening the misery.

The larger constructions were still broken and scarred from an earthquake twenty-five years earlier. Churches had lost steeples, apartment blocks and government buildings had tumbled to the ground.

There were some green areas with newly built, or freshly restored houses of Spanish design. They cringed behind high walls, embarrassed, and afraid of the poverty that surrounded them.

Ricky, who was sitting next to the window, turned to Salvadore, his mouth wide open, his little gold filling dull, almost unnoticeable in the aircraft light. '*La ciudad no tiene corazón, amigo,*' he finally managed to say. This time he used Spanish with Salvadore, but sometimes it would be Miskito. With me it was always English. Salvadore, who had been twice before to Managua to box, sympathized, 'Yeah, it's pretty ugly, but there's a lot more to do here than in Puerto Cabezas, *amigo*. Only you have to be careful.'

*

Eduardo's Managua house was made of concrete. All the houses in his area were the same. Next to this neighbourhood, on both sides, were the tin towns.

The house was full of people. It never became clear to me who they were, but it was obvious that there was no room for us. I was right, we had to sleep in another house belonging to a relation.

'But you eat with us,' Eduardo comforted, when he saw the panic on Salvadore's face.

The house we stayed in was unfinished. We slept next to cement bags on the floor and washed under a cold tap outside. Each morning while it was still dark the three of us would wake and dress, and by first light we would be running. During the day and in the late evening we would walk the streets, trying to stay cool, talking with people we didn't know who didn't seem to mind. Many knew who we were: *el Negro, el Indio e el Gringo*. They knew who Ricky had to fight, and they told us how good he was, how hard he punched, but they wished us well.

Ricky and Salvadore wouldn't allow me to go about without one of them to accompany me. 'This is a dangerous town for a gringo,' they would tell me many times. 'People have knives and guns and they are very poor.' In the afternoons we would travel to the gymnasium in trucks disguised as buses.

The Alexis Arguello Gymnasium is a large, tin structure built among the shanties. Just outside its main entrance stood a small vending cart on wheels. A young woman stood next to the fire that had been lit on the cart. She was frying banana and small pieces of pork, that was served with cabbage salad. Two young children clung tightly to her apron as she worked. Next to the cart stood a small icebox filled with cold Coca-Cola and a sweet pink drink produced locally that was very popular. Next to the icebox, on the lip of the gutter, sat a group of very drunk men.

When we entered the gym, the heat magnified by the tin roof almost overwhelmed me. In two corners fighters slammed away at heavy bags that hung from pieces of iron screwed horizontally into the wall, skipped or practised punching the *mascote*. Sweat ran in rivers, finding paths down their backs or dripping in rivulets off the end of their noses, running across their chests and soaking their pants. We were shown under the bleachers to change, and discovered yet more training space, more bags, gloves hanging by their laces on racks, stinking bandages used to protect hands drying in the airless furnace.

Preparations were under way for the big fight night. The ropes of the ring were being tightened and its canvas floor repainted with the label of the famous Mexican beer, Corona. Circles of blue and red with the gold bottle, the emblem of the company, splashed in the centre.

The ring had been fenced off to make seating room for the ringside ticket holders, but it was four days until the fights and the space was still being used as a training area. Outside the fence on all four sides were bleachers, cheap wooden seats reaching at an angle upwards towards the ceiling. People were watching the training that was going on everywhere. Old men with bent backs and scarred faces, hands still bent into fists moving with the rhythm of the action, children in school uniforms, trainers, promoters, tattooed fighters who were finished training and who could not bring themselves to leave, hoping to learn something.

There were five full-time trainers at the Alexis Arguello Gym. Each in turn came to greet us, wish us the best and offer any assistance they could. All except for one, Pepi Rodrigas, the trainer of Johnny West, Ricky's opponent. Normally even the opponent's trainer was friendly, but Pepi was just a little worm by nature. It was common knowledge, nothing personal. Each of these trainers had his own equipment, his own section where he trained his fighters. Some were doing well and had champions, others would have champions in the future.

Chocoyo, a little thickset man in his sixties with spiky grey hair and dancing eyes, was having a lean patch, training men past their best and boys doing their best with a long way to go.

Lucky Jimenez, who trained in the opposite corner of the gym, had a lot of girls in his group. 'Why do you think they call him lucky?' Chocoyo whispered to me one afternoon, almost falling from his seat, as laughter raked his body.

Juan Salinas who always wore ballet shoes when he trained his fighters, had a strong group which included two Nicaraguan champions and an amateur Central American champion. Juan was also training three boys who had just returned to Nicaragua from the United States with their parents. They came from wealthy families who had fled the country when Somoza was overthrown. They were more American than Nicaraguan, arriving in new four-wheel drives, wearing expensive clothes. Their heavy bodies looked out of place amongst the harshly-trained boxers, but it didn't matter, they didn't want to fight, they just wanted to fight against real fighters; it made them feel macho. Juan didn't care, they paid him and he gave them some of his time in exchange. Sometimes he'd get to ride in one of their jeeps.

Managua was a very poor city. There was a despair about it that was the legacy of the bloody civil war. There was little work, no money, and a lot of violence – guns that had been left over from the war were used to rob and kill. But in Alexis Arguello, where a lot of wild boys trained, the only thing that mattered was learning boxing from trainers who taught you as best they could and worried about you. Chocoyo, Lucky Jimenez, Juan Salinas, and even the little worm Pepi were in charge, and everybody knew it.

We trained Ricky and Salvadore lightly that week, mostly

skipping and working with the *mascote*. It didn't make sense – they needed to spar, to be boxing other men, but Eduardo wouldn't hear of it. He was afraid that our boys were not ready, or worse, not good enough for the Managuans. He was afraid for himself and for his own reputation. And our boys would be the ones to pay.

I had just bought sweet black coffee and pieces of sliced, thickly-buttered bread for Chocoyo and myself, from a lady in a white apron who worked in the gymnasium every afternoon. We were watching Salvadore and Ricky train and Chocoyo was giving me the benefit of '*mi experienza*', when in walked a group of men I had never seen before. A small man with a moustache and short cropped hair was being escorted or guarded by two large black men. Chocoyo called out a greeting and then explained to me that this was Rosendo, the world strawweight champion. 'A Nicaraguan,' he told me proudly. The other men were his two trainers. 'You thought they were from the coast like Ricky, eh, but they're from Panama. When a fighter gets good enough he always leave Nicaragua, there's no money here. Rosendo is in Nicaragua for a week to see his mother, then he will return to Panama City.'

Salvadore stopped skipping and let the sweat dam together, readying itself to drive down his body and puddle the floor. He turned to look at the men moving towards the dressing area. He knew who it was. He had twice boxed Rosendo in the Nicaraguan amateur finals. I could see him shake his head slowly and thoughtfully but who knows what he was thinking. And then he began his skipping again, sweat flew from his body. Chocoyo went quiet for a moment and when he spoke again he seemed to trip over the words. 'He had a real chance before the rum got him, your little Indian, but the rum finishes plenty in Nicaragua.'

In the afternoon of the day before the fight we travelled to the national sports stadium to have Ricky and Salvadore weighed. The small room was full of half-naked, hard-bodied boxers preparing to step onto the scales. Two Mexicans who had been brought down to fight two of Nicaragua's best were the first to be weighed. They were under the limit, everybody applauded. After the weigh-in a doctor in attendance checked their eyes, hands and hearts. The boxing officials recorded and controlled everything. Salvadore stepped up, no trouble, under the weight. Ricky, who had been starving all week, eating lightly and drinking very little, took his turn.

He was over. Just a few ounces, but enough to give Pepi Rodrigas, the little worm, his chance. He wouldn't accept Ricky's weight. Ricky would have to sweat some more. We ran out into the corridors and headed towards the toilets at the back of the building. We found plastic garbage bags, cut holes in the top and designed them into armless jackets, pulled them over his shoulders, and then fashioned another plastic bag on his head that resembled a Ku Klux Klan hood. And then he skipped. First ten minutes – it wasn't enough, he was still over. Five minutes more. Ricky could hardly move, he had not eaten all day. It was sad to watch, but these were the rules. On the third try he weighed in under the limit. The little worm smiled.

After the weigh-in it was straight to a restaurant in a market with tables on the street, where we watched boys with their own T-shirts tied to their heads carrying heavy bags of flour, or beans, or boxes of fruit. Crowds of people drifted by. The exhaust from the trucks that were buses choked you, and Salvadore and Ricky ate and ate. They downed two full meals of rice, fried banana, chicken and tortilla, and washed it down with two bottles of cold wonderful Victoria beer, Nicaragua's best. I had never heard of giving alcohol to boxers before a fight, but it wasn't much, and Eduardo swore that was the way it was done in Nicaragua. Salvadore sipped them slowly, savouring their effect.

*

We arrived at the stadium two hours before the fights. We were early, but Salvadore would be one of the first and we had to be ready. We stood in the early evening light on the footpath outside the stadium, escaping the heat, shuffling, waiting. Crowds of excited, expectant people arrived. Other trainers came to join us. A group of drunk men, who I learned were all ex-boxers, sat where they always sat – on the lip of the gutter next to the vending cart that sold fried banana and pork – drinking away their disappointments.

Salvadore stripped down under the bleachers amongst the training bags and hanging gloves. Other boys were getting ready, tying laces, changing into silk trunks, wrapping their hands to protect their knuckles. Groups of people were moving in and out. Fight officials hovered. Two doctors waited and watched, hoping they wouldn't be needed. Trainers and assistant trainers were everywhere. The space was long, narrow, and not very high. It was soon crowded.

Salvadore was ready. He sat calmly, red eight-ounce fighting gloves already tied to his hands. A black-and-gold silk gown draped over his shoulders to protect against a sudden chill in a changing room that had become a sauna.

The roar filled the dressing room, rushing in from the seats above our heads. A fight had ended; now it was our turn. Slowly we marched Salvadore towards the ring.

I could see the rich kids sitting in the front row, well fed and smoking large cigars. They yelled greetings in their impeccable English as we passed. I gazed around and saw that the stadium was full, not a seat left. The crowd seemed happy. They had already seen good fights and expected to see more. A large man who seemed to be a little crazy, or just drunk, was shadowboxing alone in front of one section of the bleachers. He could hardly stand. His punches were wild and uncoordinated.

215

He was laughing uncontrollably and the people cheered.

Salvadore moved well for the first two rounds. He was a southpaw – he was left-handed and – the kid that he fought seemed confused and worried. Salvadore landed a lot of good punches, but then his heart refused to pump in enough air to feed his body, to nourish his muscles. His hands fell lower, he started to be hit when he shouldn't have. His legs moved heavily. Salvadore was exhausted. We had not had enough time after his last drunk to prepare him. A clash of heads ended the fight: Salvadore was cut over the right eyebrow and the referee stopped the bout. Alcohol had beaten him again.

We worked quickly to prepare Ricky. While I cut the tape that would be moulded over Ricky's fists to protect and harden them, Eduardo wrapped, taking special care that the fingers could still be closed and the knuckles were well protected. And that the tape was not too tight so that the blood could still flow and the hands would stay awake.

Salvadore had cut away his own hand tape and was carefully tying the laces of Ricky's high white boxing boots. Chocoyo was massaging Ricky's shoulders to knead away the fear.

A large man dressed in a police uniform came towards us. As he moved to one side I could see that another man, also dressed in uniform, was following. The second man was squat, with short-cropped greying hair. He was greeted politely, respectfully as he moved through the crowd. When he reached us Eduardo and Chocoyo stopped what they were doing to welcome him. Salvadore stood up quickly, only Ricky remained seated, unable to rise because both Eduardo and Chocoyo had placed their hands on his shoulders, accepting the uniformed man's honour as a group.

The man grabbed Ricky by the hand, smiled and wished him luck. He then leaned closer to Ricky, letting go of his hand and

216

placing his own on Ricky's head. '*Pelear bien para la Costa, eso es muy importante,*' he whispered.

His name was Commissioner Dean Dixon, and like Ricky he was a black man from the Caribbean coast, a '*Costeno*'. Chocoyo told me that he was the second most powerful police officer in Nicaragua, a Sandinista, one of the few from the coast. '*Un hombre muy fuerte.*'

'And the other man who led him in?' I asked.

'Hah,' Chocoyo replied, 'that's the mule that pulls the cart, his bodyguard.'

'He's very important to us, to Ricky,' Eduardo said excitedly to me, wiping the sweat from his nose with the back of his sleeve and draping his hand around my shoulder as he watched the commissioner leave to take his seat. 'He loves boxing and the police control two boxing gymnasiums. If Ricky does well he'll accept him here in Managua. They will pay for his training, his living. He will have the chance to fight often, to go places, or no place. This is his one chance in life. Poor boys like him don't get two.'

Johnny West stood in his corner waiting silently for the bell to sound. He was taller than Ricky with much heavier muscles, a fine long nose, and high chiselled cheekbones that showed Indian blood. He had a light honey colour and sharp green eyes that should have belonged to someone else. His short, curly dark hair was worn like a helmet cut high over the ears. Pepi Rodrigas stood in front of him, instructing and threatening.

We worked on Ricky, greasing his eyebrows, nose and shoulders, trying to put enough Vaseline on to help the punches slide away without bringing it to the notice of the referee. We rubbed him and talked to him. We could do no more, he was ready.

From the sound of the bell that called round one, we could see that it would not be easy. West was not a straight fighter. A lot of his punches were round and should have been easy to block, but they were fast elusive punches. West would often feint or trick before throwing them. He moved well – lightly and sweetly – but it was his strength that was beating us. Ricky would block, yet still be stunned and hurt. Ricky should have been able to punch through the centre, but his arms had been hit mercilessly. They had lost their power and wanted only to defend: they had no confidence to attack.

Still Ricky boxed bravely, moving forward whenever he could, occasionally hurting West with a straight right hand that would catch him coming in, overconfident, with his hands held low. His left found West's nose and mouth with regularity, forcing him to spit blood, soiling his chest. But nothing stopped the attack, the punishment. In the fourth round Ricky went down.

The referee counted slowly to seven before Ricky stood unsteadily. He looked apologetically towards our corner and then to the referee who had taken him by the wrists and was carefully cleaning his gloves that had been dirtied by the canvas. He was asked whether he could continue. Ricky nodded fiercely and the fight began again.

Ricky was desperate to win and he began to fight with a passion, driving West back onto the ropes with lefts and rights that had found speed and power through the humiliation of near defeat. Johnny moved backwards inelegantly, hands held high, trying to deflect the scything gloves and the unending storm of punches. Sometimes West would land, but he couldn't fight his way off the ropes or stop Ricky's charge. West landed a right that slowed Ricky for a moment, surprised him, but didn't hurt him. The referee rushed in between the two fighters and, placing his forearms on their sweating slippery chests, holding them apart, stopped the contest. Ricky turned towards us in confusion. West's hand was raised in victory.

The crowd that had been yelling, cheering, screaming loudly, fell silent. They were as confused as Ricky, as we all were. But only for a moment.

West was the local favourite, everybody loved him, but this was no victory and the fight crowd was not going to stand for it, we weren't going to stand for it. A madness took the public and they started to roar, howl and whistle their disapproval. They stamped their feet, they stood punching the air with closed fists. Eduardo, Chocoyo and I rushed towards the judges, pleading for Ricky, threatening in exasperation. The boxing officials joined us and it was quickly decided it had been wrong. We agreed that it would be declared a no decision contest, a draw. They would have to fight again another day. The madness faded.

The crazy man was again boxing shadows. Living in his imagination, happy, but the crowds had left and there was nobody to applaud him. Commissioner Dean Dixon leaned against the bar that was still open because he still wanted to drink, and watched and watched. His bodyguard shook his head in disgust, a policeman's intolerant disgust.

'Ricky fought well,' the commissioner finally said to no one in particular, sipping from his whisky that was still almost full and was not his first. Eduardo caressed his glass of cola with his small thick hands, melting the ice that floated like icebergs around the rim of the glass, and waited patiently for Dixon to continue. I called Ricky over to listen; it was about him.

The wind blew fiercely from the north, coming across the sea, pushing darkness towards Puerto Cabeza's small airport. Sheets of rain slammed into the gravel and churned it into pebble-textured mud. The Managua–Puerto Cabezasplane turned off the asphalt runway onto the dirt and taxied slowly through the newly-born puddles to the shed that served as ticket office, waiting room and bar. Ricky waited until the engine had been cut and the propellers had died before rising from his stool to begin his walk through the downpour towards the plane. Salvadore, bleary-eyed, saying nothing, reached between his legs for the bottle from which he had been sipping since arriving at the airfield. He then followed unsteadily.

It had been two weeks since the fights in Managua and a week since Commissioner Dean Dixon had called the post office in Puerto Cabezas to leave the message that he had arranged for both Ricky and Salvadore to live and train in Managua. The message continued that their families must remain in Puerto Cabezas but they would be given money to live on while their men were away.

Ricky, smiling, turned to wave goodbye to us before bending his head to enter the tiny plane. His white clothes were plastered to his body, his hair beads sparkled from the wetness. Salvadore tripped as he stepped into the Cessna and fell to his knees. When he tried to rise he lurched drunkenly, grabbing wildly at another passenger. They both fell to the muddy ground. The pilot refused to let him board the plane that would take him to the capital.

Salvadore, the Fighting Miskito, was never again invited to train in Managua. He remains living with his wife and children in a small, unpainted wooden hut which he shares with two other families. He earns an unreliable living in construction, and carting and carrying produce in the market. He still drinks. Ricky won the Central American lightweight title in his ninth contest. Along the way he defeated Johnny West. A world title shot is expected in the near future.

ME AND CHARLIE BROWN

Darryl Wallace, whose nom de guerre was Charlie Brown, trained with his mate Dave Agnew, a twisted-nosed, Newcastle junior welterweight for six years. They sparred together every day. When Dave died of an overdose of cocaine, administered with a needle by a strung-out pusher, Charlie cornered the man in a night club and waited. When the bouncers tried to hunt Charlie away, he stood his ground

'You were going to kill him, Charlie?' I asked, looking into dark eyes set deep inside swollen disfigured eyebrows, ignoring the noise that came from the other drinkers.

Charlie smiled and lifted the schooner of beer to his mouth, froth caught the tip of his moustache, liquid spilled from the glass, dribbling through his coarse thick beard.

'No, I was only going to bash the cock, I couldn't kill anybody.'

'Did you get him?' I asked.

An old man passed, hesitated, smiled with grey disfigured teeth, then patted Charlie warmly on the back with a hand covered in wrinkled opaque skin. 'You're a dead set ringer for your grandfather, Charlie,' he said, and moved slowly on.

Charlie nodded, showing a small diamond set in a front tooth and framed in white gold, 'All the old buggers say that to me,' and continued, 'He wouldn't come out, the cock. Stayed drinking inside with the bouncers. It didn't matter, later he went to jail and somebody killed him inside.'

I had lived overseas for twenty-five years, and this was the first time we had shared a beer together in all that time. Charlie took me to his local: a sandstone pub built on a corner, set on a hill. Before we pushed through its front doors we both glanced eastwards, over bush, past bluffs and cliffs to the Pacific Ocean miles away.

Charlie stood up and walked away from the bar, played absent-mindedly with his dark, shoulder-length ponytail: pulling it tight at the back of his head, outlining high sharp cheekbones, the flat twisted nose, and the scars above the eyes that I hadn't noticed before, wriggled a hand in his pocket and pulled out his cigarettes – Benson and Hedges – the same brand he had smoked all those years ago.

'It's the law, you have ta stand a metre and a half from the bar so the barmaid don't get cancer,' he drawled when he saw me staring, and stood there in a cloud of smoke.

It was the same Charlie I thought, the strong little bloke who walked into the tin shed that early evening all those years ago, standing first in the doorway, hesitating, looking around, letting his eyes rest on each of us, finally nodding slowly as we nodded to him. Moving among the bags and balls, fingering the hard broken gloves, noticing the small roped square that we used for sparring, waiting for the order to strip and train as a boxer for the very first time. The one who was loyal to his mates. The shed at the back of the house was a professional boxing gymnasium, and Charlie was to become its star.

It was late afternoon, knock off time, and the pub which like so many in Australia these days had been preened and polished, was filling with drinkers. I ordered two more beers, sipping mine at the head, holding it to my mouth, gazing over the glass, taking in the Heritage green walls, the timber bar, the chest-high timber tables, the unused fireplace, a large mirror decorated with a frosted image of the hotel, old photos showing the hotel when it was a plain brick structure, and the coal mine that had been closed for thirty years and whose workers used the hotel as their second home. It had been turned into an English tavern I thought, disappointed, desperate for the places of my youth, when Australian pubs were great open spaces of cold tile cut through by massive long bars, when walls were dotted with dartboards and covered with photos of rugby league greats; racehorses crossing finishing posts; greyhounds, at full stretch, dragging their tongues as they chased uncatchable hares.

When I told this to Charlie he answered, 'Same type of drinkers but,' as if to lessen my disappointment. And when I looked around, needing to confirm Charlie's observation, I saw gangs of road workers, builders, miners and mechanics. There were neatly dressed office workers, paunchy and loud, fitting in like an important piece of a jigsaw puzzle. Old men, creased and lined, sat sipping schooners near the window, arms folded across their chests, drifting at times as if communicating with the wandering souls of dead mates who had spent a good part of their lives sitting in their company. And I was pacified. This was Charlie's territory, where he had been raised, where the hard bastards came from.

I had wanted to find Charlie again because I needed to talk. I wanted to hear about his glory, because in some way it reflected on me, because I had been there at the start, and because I had fought him. I hoped his company, our history, Charlie's words would somehow redeem me. I had promised more, you see, much more than I achieved and this haunted me.

'Hey, Charlie, there's a sheila looking for ya.'

Charlie smiled at me with bare arms folded over his chest like the old blokes near the window. 'Yeah, that's her there,' he said nodding in my direction, bringing a queer look to the face of the big man who had said it. (My mother had placed an ad in a newspaper, 'Looking for old boxing mate, Charlie Brown,' and the big man had answered it. He had been one of three men who had called my mother, happy they knew where to find Charlie.)

'I lived on eight hundred calories a day for years,' Charlie began again, reaching for another cigarette, but giving up when he realized he'd have to walk away again. 'I'd get up in the morning, eat nothing, go for a run, then go to work painting houses, keep going through morning tea and lunch, finish early, and go straight to the gym, and train until seven at night. And then I'd come home and eat boiled vegetables and drink black tea. When my missus was home to make it, which wasn't very often,' he added as an afterthought.

'Sugar?' I asked.

'No sugar, just black tea. But then I got smart, and just stopped eating for three days before a fight. It worked the same.'

I knew Charlie had fought most of his fights in a division that was much lighter than his natural weight. And I knew Charlie had finally left his first missus, a Catholic girl he had been with since she was twelve years old, and got another.

'You remember much about our fight?'

But before I could remember, a group of men shouted a greeting to Charlie from across the bar, Charlie waved back, rubbing at his swollen battered eyebrow with the palm of his hand, before folding his waving arm again with the other and resting it across his chest.

And then it came back to me as if it was yesterday. It was the first time that my mother had seen me fight. I had boxed ten times as an amateur, winning all of them, and this was my fourth professional fight. But it wasn't a real fight.

My opponent hadn't turned up, something had happened. Our trainer, who was also the promoter of the boxing evening, told me I would be fighting Charlie in a six-round fight. It was a full house and we would be paid sixty dollars each: that was a week's wages in those days, how could you say no?

It was held at Newcastle West Leagues club, and the ring had been set up in the main auditorium. The tables in the hall were swamped in beer glasses, all the seats were full. Cigarette smoke lingered under the lights, drifting to form a grey gossamer cloud.

I remembered landing my heavy punches on his chest and arms, and in the final three-minute round, after fifteen minutes of hard but controlled boxing, we tore into each other. I think that we both had a sense that the punters deserved a little more, and we gave it to them. And we brought them to their feet, making them spill their beer, filling the whole place with a roar. Causing my mother to stand and shout as if only her voice could help me.

'I didn't want to fight you,' Charlie said, bringing me back to the present. 'It wasn't right training together and then having to fight each other. Our trainer earned off both of us that night, and he had a full fight card. We got the fight of the night but.'

'I'd forgotten,' I answered, 'but I do remember that a big shower of coins was thrown into the ring, and you blackened both of my eyes. Also that my mother was pretty angry at you.'

'Aw yeah, but you were a very good boxer, cock, a better boxer than me, a classy boxer, a very classy boxer, I had to get inta ya but.

'And I had to fight more stews after you,' Charlie continued, warming to the subject, 'and plenty a times I had to fight blokes a lot heavier like this bloke in Thailand called Muangsurin, he was a lightweight, three weight divisions heavier than me, the cock, and he was hard. And I had to fight when I was not trained right. It was good money, but it wasn't right.

'Trainers always look out for themselves,' Charlie continued, strangely unangered by the subject, as if that was the fate of all fighters. 'One time we went up ta fight in Port Moresby in New Guinea. I fought a bloke called Tiger Mann in an eight-rounder, how he could hit – hardest puncher I ever fought,' Charlie added, blowing air through pursed lips as if that somehow softened the memory of the punches. 'He knocked me down in the second round, we fought a draw but.

'Dave, my mate that died of the drug overdose, he fought up there too, a bloke from Bougainville, a heavy puncher, way too good. Dave took a bashing from him, a bad bashing, that wasn't right. It was his last fight before he died. Yeah, the cocks just look out for themselves, they don't give a fuck, do they?' he finished, asking for my confirmation, leaving me nodding slowly back.

Charlie stood, still thinking about the wild boy from the New Guinea bush who had a punch in either hand, or about his mate who died a senseless death, or about trainers and promoters who didn't care, walked a metre and a half away and lit up another Benson and Hedges. Another man came to join him and I was left with my own thoughts:

In my third fight my opponent had twenty-nine professional fights, but I can't even remember his name, and then after Charlie, it was an Aboriginal boy from Redfern in Sydney called Stevie Wonder, and my last three fights were all against Jimmy Boyle, the former Australian amateur champion. When they announced him, they always added, 'Undefeated in three years.' In our final fight he beat me so badly that for days afterwards people moved away from me when I passed, shocked by my swollen, blackened eyes, the cut, protruding lip, and the nose that seemed twice as big as it should have. It was a six-rounder and he battered me while I stood against the ropes taking everything he had to throw. I had been promised a main event if I won.

'Donny.' It was Charlie calling me – I had fought under the name Donny Leslie. Charlie broke through the old voices in my head that made no sound, but caused the veins in my temples to swell to near bursting, and my heart to pound as if it might explode my chest. I stared at nothing, concentrating on something that happened so long ago and could not be changed, as if I were an idiot or experiencing the first stages of Alzheimer's.

'Donny,' he called again before I was fully recovered. We walked together outside the pub. The light was failing, greying and dulling the buildings. Charlie pointed across the road with a stump of a cigarette. We were looking at another pub, a brick place painted khaki green.

'That's the Ocean View. If you like heavy metal, bikers, and blokes with pins in their tongues and noses, and sheilas with pins in other places, it's a good place to drink. Next time we'll go and have a beer there. My great-uncles won it in a card game, that was a long time ago but. They were my mother's brothers, the hard side of the family, all coal miners, the lot of them. They useta ride pushbikes to work.'

'As were my family, and they rode pushbikes too,' I reminded him.

'Yeah, Dudley coal miners were different to Cessnock coal miners but – they all had two heads up your way.'

'What about these uncles?' I asked, adding that he better not bring up the two-headed thing around Cessnock.

Charlie sucked deeply on the dregs of his cigarette, blinking repeatedly as the smoke caught his eyes, coughing lightly as it swirled through his throat, finally throwing the butt on top of a beer keg that that had been chained outside the entrance to the pub, and finished his story. 'They closed it down, drank it dry, and then gave it back to the owner.' His eyes pinched together at the memory, his lips pulled back, almost unnoticeable under the beard. I realized that pride was rushing through his body.

When we returned to the bar, Linsay, the proprietor of our pub, came and stood beside us.

'Charlie, somebody is looking for you,' he said, towering over us, tall and weathered, strong, commanding, respectful.

Charlie smiled at me again. 'This is Donny.'

'We trained together,' I added.

'You're a fighter too?' he asked.

'Well, not like Charlie,' I answered quickly. 'I took plenty of hidings, got out after eight fights, no not like Charlie.'

'You were a classy boxer but. If you had of been trained and managed right, you would have gone as far as me. You weren't trained or managed right.'

Three new beers were ordered, a roar came from the corner of the pub, Linsay looked up, concerned about order, but it was only a roar of exuberance. Following Linsay's gaze, I noticed for the first time a surfboard mounted on a wall, and while still wondering how I could have missed it, spotted the autographed picture of Joe Cocker behind the bar. The feeling of drinking in an English tavern faded.

'I fought Steve Walker for the Australian title on September 2nd, 1975,' Charlie began again, when he saw that he had our attention. 'I had already fought him seven times. He won most of those on points. This was a three-minute round fight but, and I'm a three-minute round fighter. That separates the men from the boys. He was good, always gave a tough fight, I stopped him in the ninth round but.'

Later I read an article, a round by round description of the fight. There were words that caught my attention and held my memory, like 'wild', 'savage', 'intelligent', but a complete paragraph stuck with me: 'Charlie and Steve stand with arms about each other's shoulders. Despite the withering ferocity of all their meetings, they have remained good cobbers. Their combats exemplify the courage and honour this most ancient and dangerous art is founded upon. All the fans at the castle salute Steve and Charlie.'

'People threw more than one hundred dollars into the ring after that fight, they said it was the greatest they'd seen in thirty-five years.'

'Who fought thirty-five years ago?' I wanted to know.

'Dunno,' answered Charlie, reaching for his cigarettes again.

'Did you ever get hurt?' I asked before he stood to smoke, thinking about my own medically diagnosed brain damage that had come from a blow to the side of my head from a bar stool swung by a skinhead in London in 1978. Or from the knockdowns and beatings I got while boxing.

'Nah, clear as a bell, never forget anything, bad eyes but, had to have two eye operations. They put a moveable stitch in an eye muscle that was damaged and pulled it back in place, but it's not evenly matched with the other muscles, and when I put my head a certain way I see double, and sometimes when I'm driving I see double, but I know the bottom picture is the right one, so no worries. It's all in the game.

'I had rheumatic fever when I was eleven years old – it gave me an odd heartbeat and bad arthritis. Had to put my hands in hot water on winter mornings just so I could open them, boxing cured me. Stopped me from fighting in the street too. Useta fight five times a week once, never lost in the street but, no rules. I'd reckon boxing was good for my health.'

Linsay, who had been listening, saying nothing, asked suddenly, 'How old are you now, Charlie?'

'Fifty,' answered Charlie, 'but I feel thirty,' he quickly added. 'I can still spar for a half an hour with good young blokes. I still wear them out.'

229

And I remembered his terrific condition when he was fighting, and when I asked him once, he told me it was because of the slow heartbeat caused by the rheumatic fever, and because he always stopped smoking ten minutes before a fight, fifteen if it was a fifteen-rounder.

'Fifty, fuck, and you didn't say anything to me.'

Charlie cocked his head to one side and raised up his shoulders as Linsay disappeared towards the back of the pub, leaving his beer on the bar. 'I've got to write you a poem,' he called back over his shoulder, oblivious to his duties as owner of the Royal Crown Hotel.

Charlie read it first, gave a cheeky grin, exposing his diamond. 'Linsay wrote a poem about Mohammad Ali once, sent it to him and got a reply, now he's a poet.' He then handed it to me.

On the eastern fringe of Newcastle, near to Dudley town,
Is a slippery little bastard, name of Charlie Brown,
Now you might see young Charlie, he's fifty now says he,
young Charlie is a part of Local Boxing History,
So don't say nothing clever about his pigtail for a laugh,
Or by the time you crack the joke you'll end up on your arse,
So don't make the error of insulting Charlie Brown,
Or he'll slowly get up off his seat and knock you quickly
     down.

Linsay
proprietor Royal Crown Hotel.

Charlie's youngest son Steven collected us from the pub. We raced back to his house on the edge of the town, beating lights, hugging corners, disregardful of police, disdainful of personal safety. Steven was eighteen and was sure as hell Charlie's boy. 'He's a rap singer,' Charlie slurred, Steve nodded in agreement.

Charlie's wife Linda fed us with chops and mash, hovering, balancing Charlie's other life with her own stories of how they had met on a blind date and how she thought him too rough, but had no choice in the end because he had kidnapped her, admitting later that she had not wanted to escape. And how Charlie had insulted her mother who was Italian, by refusing to eat the meal of spaghetti she had cooked for him. Charlie, who had just fought and had been starving himself to make the boxing weight, told her he was going out for some real food.

'I wanted to eat ice cream and cakes and the cunt,' Charlie began to explain.

'Don't use that word here,' Linda stopped him, brushing back her dark thick hair, but with no anger showing on her face that had changed little from the twenty-year-old photograph on the mantelpiece.

'The count without the o,' Charlie shot back, 'and I still don't like spaghetti.'

I heard how he called her a wog, and how she called him a bloody kangaroo, and how they still didn't talk, even though she had come to live with them. When I told him how my mother-in-law hardly spoke to me the first year that I lived with her daughter, all Charlie said was 'See, Linda . . .'

Charlie lit a Benson and Hedges and was ordered from the room. 'Linda don't understand that passive smoking makes you immune to cancer,' Charlie informed me, dragging out the word immune, making it sound twice as long, before rising and moving to stand in a doorway that led to an outside patio, his bare arms folded against the cold, his cigarette burning brightly as if its fire was being stoked. Wind drifted through the opening causing their pet parakeet to chatter frantically.

When Charlie's two older sons visited, their mother offered them food, admonished them when they swore, ordered them outside when they tried to smoke, adored them. The oldest boy, who had the dark, round, unlined face of his mother and who wore his thick brown hair long like his father, told how he had his arm broken by the police when they twisted it to make an arrest. It had only been for spinning the wheels of his car.

'Coppers can be bastards around here,' Charlie confirmed, 'some of them are all right but.' And then I heard stories of Charlie's own run-ins with them, but again it was only because a seat belt had not been used, or a driver's licence had been forgotten. Linda listened quietly while Charlie told how he had given coppers a hard time, smiling, shaking her head, looking at me as if for an ally. It was the smile of a woman who had lived for years in a house with men she still didn't understand, but I knew that I couldn't make it any clearer to her. I knew she would never accept that it was simply about not being taken without a fight, and that for some men there was no other way.

The other son, named David after Charlie's mate Dave Agnew, was just twenty and awaiting the birth of his second child. He was Charlie's hope for carrying on the boxing tradition. 'I taught all the boys to fight. David, he's never been beaten on the street, he thinks like me.'

And when you looked at him you could sense Charlie's fearlessness, his hardness – although it was well disguised under a mantle of charm and sincere manners. But when I asked him whether he wanted to box, he was unsure, and when I asked their mother, she answered. 'Look at their faces, they're all too pretty.' And then I asked her whether she had watched Charlie fight and she told me how anxiety caused her to bring up blood when she did.

After the boys left, Charlie showed me round the house: the floor-to-ceiling boxing ball that was set in a doorway and compelled you to weave or punch to get around it, and the boxing bags hanging in the garage among the lawnmowers, motorbikes, and garden tools. He told me about the local kids he was training, 'Not to fight but, I just teach them to handle themselves,' and about the boxing club he had set up in the Philippines with other members of the Australian boxing community.

I told him about the boxing club I had built in Nicaragua and we agreed that we had started the clubs for the same reasons – to give the kids a place to go, some direction and discipline, a chance at something. Our clubs had even suffered the same fate; all the gloves, bags and skipping ropes had been stolen. In Nicaragua my ring had vanished without trace, piece by piece. But the clubs had had a life, and made a difference for a short while, and we both agreed that when you're so poor it's hard to resist all that brightly-coloured new leather, especially when it was paid for by a rich westerner who can afford to pay for it again.

After my tour, we settled in front of the television to watch one of Charlie's old fights. As the tape began to rewind noisily, slowly on his old machine, Charlie reached for a Benson and Hedges, thought better of it, and waited impatiently, while I studied a black-and-white photograph hanging on the wall. It was Charlie, hair flying, throwing an awkward right uppercut at the chin of a fighter called Peter Mitrevski.

'I still hate the cock,' he began, nodding at the picture on the wall. 'He head butted me and cut my eye when I fought him for the Australian bantamweight title. They stopped the fight in the eighth round, that robbed me of the title. I fought him three times altogether, he did the same every time. He's a dirty fighter.'

'So there he was, all pale and furry faced and stringy and mean-eyed like an old weasel with a burr in its backside, smashing his gloves together, barely able to wait to get at Mitrevski.' This is how Jeff Wells, writing in *The Australian*, described Charlie at the start

233

of their third meeting. But I would read that later. 'Did you hate everybody you fought?'

'No, sweet people most of them. I took it easy on some of the fighters I fought, they was only trying to earn a living. Jimmy Bowen came and stayed here a couple of times after our fight.' (When I read about the fight with Jimmy Bowen that Charlie had lost on a split decision for the Australian Junior featherweight title over fifteen three-minute rounds, it was recounted as a two-man war, and as the best fight ever held in Newcastle. One writer wrote: 'It was one of those fights that live with you – move right in with you, and take up permanent residence in your memory.') 'Jimmy's real quiet, didn't drink much when he was here, we mostly argued about who won the fight. I still think I won it, knocked him down twice, Jimmy's sure he won it. Jimmy's a real sweet man. I beat him but.'

A bottle of beer miraculously appeared at my feet, Charlie fell back onto the lounge beside me. The fight flickered into life. Two small, hard men, one almost too dark for the camera to focus on, began moving lightly towards each other across the lighted square canvas, and then exploded, blending into a melee of lethal punching.

'He's Indonesian, the cunt, his name is Didik Mulyardi, he was rated number eight in the world. We were supposed to fight in Surabaya, but the police came into our hotel and told us that the fight was off because the Chinese mafia had just shot dead the promoter over some counterfeit money. And then they told us that if the fight went on and I won, the Indonesians would shoot me, and if I lost, the Chinese would shoot me, the cunts. My new trainer, the old pommy cunt, wanted to go home, but I wasn't going without my money.'

I sipped at the beer that fell heavily onto a full stomach. Linda sat quietly by the dining table reading, disregarding us entirely. The cat still slinked hopefully around us.

'They moved us out of the hotel at midnight and drove us for two hours to another town.'

'Where?' I asked.

'I don't remember the name,' he answered, shaking his head, drank thirstily as if his memory needed sustenance, glanced at the television screen, seeing himself at war, blew air from pursed lips as he always did when trying to ward off the memory of hard punches and said, 'Whatever I hit him with he just kept coming, he's the toughest man I ever fought.' He paused again to blow more air through pursed lips, and continued.

'I was over there with two other boxers, Glen Hillier was one of them, he was a good mate of mine, Glen's dead now too.' Charlie paused a moment, nodded his head a few times, fixing his thoughts on his old mate. 'He was working on his own truck when it ran over him,' (answering my question before I'd asked it.) 'We useta have a bit of fun with the locals after training, I'd lead Glen around on a dog chain and he'd be growling at the crowd. Sometimes I'd throw him dog biscuits.'

The fight took on an extra ferocity. The two men had stopped slipping punches, there was no more bobbing or weaving, no more concern for defence, their feet were planted, and all their punches were thrown with shoulder and weight behind them, from all angles, but with speed and calamitous control. Charlie suddenly doubled over, his gloved hands reaching between his own legs.

'The cock hit me in the balls.'

When they came together again, I saw Charlie's head slam into Mulyardi, a look of pain and shock flushing his face, and the next round it looked as if Charlie bit into Mulyardi's shoulder, the shock and pain returning to the face of the Indonesian.

'Yeah, and I growled like a dog after I bit him,' Charlie confirmed.

It was the eighth round when Charlie went down, came up on

one knee, stood, but was not allowed to continue by the referee. He protested, trying to get around the referee, wanting to reach Didik Mulyardi one more time.

'He hit me in the guts and I nearly shit myself. We had all had diarrhoea from that Indonesian food. All of us were dehydrated. That cock of a referee did me a favour.'

That night I slept at Charlie's and Linda's. A bed was made up for me in Linda's computer room. A sketch of a well-muscled naked man with three heads hung on the wall. It was a pen drawing of Charlie by Linda. I woke agitated and unsure of where I was. The howling of their cat on the balcony outside my window startled me out of a restless sleep. I showered under cold water – my way of fighting a hangover – dressed and wandered into the living room. The wind was banging a door that had not been closed, carrying with it an early morning spring chill. Save for the door it was very quiet. Even the birds still slept.

Newspaper reports of Charlie's fights lay scattered about the floor. I had glanced at them the night before, but it had been late when Charlie brought them out. I now read slowly, aware that my head was banging slightly, knowing that my brains needed time to absorb information. It was a history of fifteen years of mayhem and unyielding battle, each page reminding you with just a few words: 'waged a memorable fight;' 'wild-eyed'; 'no let up'; 'a hard one'; 'Charlie loses a rough'un'; 'rabbit punching', 'kicking'; 'calculating ferocity'; 'fought like barrelled wildcats'; 'mighty heart'; 'Charlie Brown fights five times with a broken shoulder.'

I hardly noticed when Charlie came into the room.

'Coffee?'

'Love some,' I answered gratefully, as he headed towards the kitchen.

'How do you fight with a broken shoulder?' I asked.

Charlie grunted, not looking at me, concentrating, spooning two equal portions of coffee out of a jar into two mugs, and then answered as he filled the water jug.

'I broke it in a car accident driving down to Sydney to fight Jimmy Bowen. It kept me out of the fight game for six months, then I fought again, but the cunt was still bad and I had to take a year off. Then I went back into training and fought five times, but it still weren't right, so I had it X-rayed again and they found that it hadn't knitted properly. It never really got right again. I retired for three years because of it. Got a big payout from the government but.'

Charlie watched the jug intently as he continued. 'When I went to court, the judge asked me how I could have all them fights if my shoulder was no good, and I told him I had to throw more right hands. It was the truth – it hurt every time I punched with the left. I fought the last six years like that, but ya have ta compensate, don't ya? It's all in the mind but. I believe you can do just about anything if you've got your mind set right.'

We sat outside by Charlie's swimming pool that was swamped with dead winter leaves to drink our coffee. The wind that crept into the house was shunted around us by a high fence. Charlie pondered, sipping his coffee, smoking contentedly, at times shaping his beard with his free hand. 'I useta throw the kids in the pool before they could swim,' he suddenly exclaimed. 'I knew they'd come up when they needed to breathe. You've got to toughen them, haven't ya?'

'Do you still miss the fighting?' I asked, sipping my coffee, happy that Charlie Brown was not my father.

He answered quickly and without consideration. 'I'd fight again tomorrow if I could, still had two titles when they forced me to retire. I was thirty-five, still strong but.'

It was then that I knew – although I think I had always known:

Charlie could have been right, maybe I would have gone a long way if I had been trained differently, managed right. I had good fast hands, a real hard right, and I'd fight, but that wasn't enough to go all the way. I could never have given myself so completely over to the fight game, never have starved myself for so long, or fronted up to spar the thousands of rounds Charlie did, or pick myself up after losing split decisions over fifteen three-minute rounds to come back just as ready the next time. I could never have survived the mismatches and sacrifices Charlie had to make for his trainers. I never loved the fighting enough, never had Charlie's true grit.

I left after breakfast. Charlie and Linda walked me down to the car, Charlie still hugging his bare arms against the cold. 'You're a sweet man,' he said to me before I left.

As I drove back towards my home in the Hunter Valley coalfields I passed along the edge of a lake. The dark midday clouds shadowed the water, blackening the surface. The wind, which had strengthened since morning, chopped and pushed the waves, churning them into a hoard of hysterical white-capped marionettes.

I pulled over but didn't leave the car, fearful of the wind, preferring warmth. Sport fishermen fleeing the weather hauled their boats awkwardly from the confused water. Pelicans, comical and persistent, bobbed unsinkable under the low sky, waiting for a handout, refusing to give up hope. I reached into the back seat of my car and collected the papers that Charlie had given me just before I left his house. It was his record and it had been compiled by Ray Mitchell, one of Australia's most respected boxing figures:

'Charlie Brown, real name Darryl Wallace, born January 31, 1953. Total bouts 62 over a period of fifteen years. Held the Australian flyweight championship between 1975 and 1977. Boxed eight more times for Australian titles in three different weight divisions. Contested the Commonwealth flyweight title against Stephen Bell in May 1976, drawing over fifteen rounds. Still held two state titles at time of retirement. Fought overseas four times: I always found Charlie to be a clean fighter, aggressive, courageous, loved to fight, heart as big as his chest and abdomen. A walk up tough fighter, and an intelligent man. Ray Mitchell.' A record to be proud of, I thought, a recommendation to cherish.

Charlie was almost thirty-six when he had his last fight. It was for the Australian Bantamweight title and he was beaten on points over twelve rounds by a nineteen-year-old kid called Kevin Johnson. After the announcement had been made, Charlie was almost in tears. Not because he had lost, or because he was badly battered, but because it was over.

I threw the papers onto the back seat and looked again towards the empty water that pounded the shore with small wild waves like an army of incensed, indefatigable flyweights. Suddenly, shamefully, I remembered how I had drunkenly complained to Charlie the night before that I had nothing to be proud of in my life. Charlie had answered truthfully, 'Ya fought me, didn't ya?'